A Very Merry Paper

CHRISTMAS

LARK
New York

New York

An Imprint of Sterling Publishing Co., Inc.
1166 Avenue of the Americas
New York, NY 10036

ISBN 978-1-4547-0880-3

Distributed in Canada by Sterling Publishing Co., Inc.
c/o Canadian Manda Group, 664 Annette Street
Toronto, Ontario, Canada M6S 2C8
Distributed in the United Kingdom by GMC Distribution Services
Castle Place, 166 High Street, Lewes, East Sussex, England BN7 1XU

For information about custom editions, special sales, and premium and corporate purchases,
please contact Sterling Special Sales at 800-805-5489 or specialsales@sterlingpublishing.com.

Manufactured in China

2 4 6 8 10 9 7 5 3 1

sterlingpublishing.com
larkcrafts.com

PHOTOGRAPHY by Chris Bain
ILLUSTRATIONS by Orrin Lundgren and Alexis Seabrook
DESIGN by Karla Baker

A Very Merry Paper

CHRISTMAS

25 CREATIVE ORNAMENTS & DECORATIONS

LARK

New York

Contents

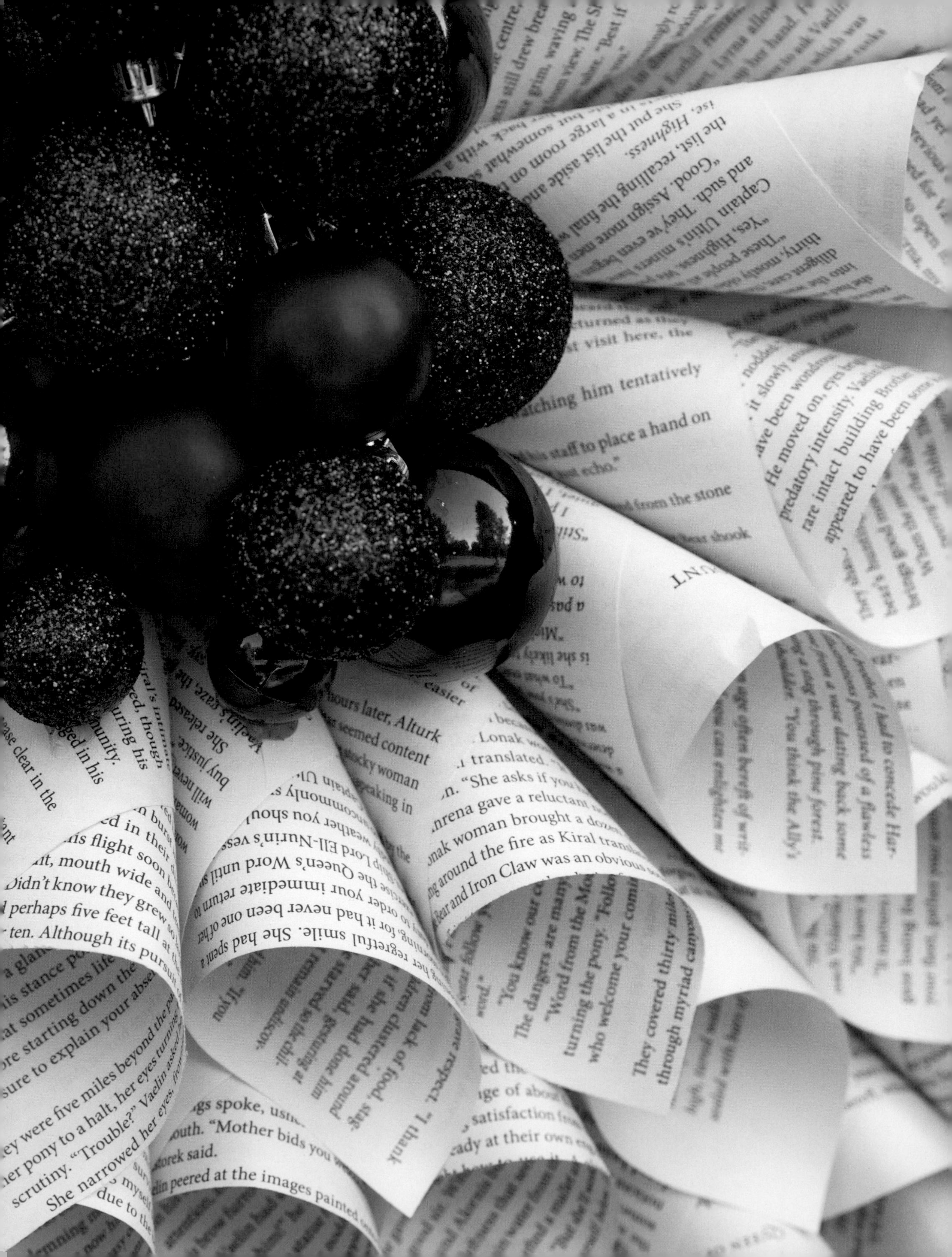

Introduction

Christmas and crafting go hand in hand. Homemade decorations from popcorn chains to handmade cards can help the holidays to feel even more festive and build warm memories of creation and celebration. The items in this book are all wonderful to make for your own home or to give as gifts. Whether shared with loved ones or used as decor, they are sure to become a beloved part of your annual tradition.

Every project in this book can be made in a weekend. Some might only take an hour while others are more involved, but they all promise to whip up more quickly than an afghan or a cross-stitched picture! It is possible to make all of these projects with supplies you can find in your home office.

Get creative and put your own spin on the projects that follow. Half of the fun that comes with crafting is customizing projects to fit your specifications. Change the colors or patterns, make elements bigger or smaller, add more glitter or take some away—it's up to you. The important part is to have fun!

Basics

In a pinch, you can craft most of the projects in this book with supplies from your office, but for the most professional results, using the right tools and supplies is important. If you're heading to the craft store, fill your craft drawer with the best tools you can find. Especially with cutting tools, investing a bit more now will really pay off when it comes to the longevity and quality of your materials.

Paper

CARDSTOCK

Look for cardstock that is pigmented all the way through each sheet. Some stock is colored only on the surface, and when cut, a white core will show through, resulting in a messy finished project.

OLD BOOKS

Old hardcover books can be found cheaply at garage sales. You might even have a novel on your shelf that you know you'll never read again. Old stories can find a new life as treasured heirloom decorations.

SCRAPBOOK PAPER

Available in large 12" × 12" pads and in loose sheets, most scrapbook paper has patterning on both sides of each sheet. When choosing paper, think about whether your finished project will allow both sides of the paper to show, and choose your patterns and colors carefully.

Cutting Tools

CIRCLE CUTTER

This luxury craft item makes cutting perfect circles accurate and easy.

CRAFT KNIFE

Buy a high-quality knife, and change out the blades as they become dull. A sharper knife is actually safer to work with because you won't have to force it through your paper. Forcing a dull knife can cause your hand to jerk and skip, making accidental injury much more likely.

GUILLOTINE PAPER CUTTER

A guillotine cutter measures and cuts perfectly straight lines. For cutting many shapes at once, a guillotine can make your work faster and more precise.

SCISSORS

A good pair of titanium scissors in a small size is invaluable for achieving precise cuts.

SELF-HEALING CUTTING MAT

It is vital to have a large, sturdy, self-healing cutting mat to work on. These are the only viable surfaces for cutting with a craft knife, and built-in measuring lines provide a great work surface for many additional crafts. Acrylic paint and glue can be easily wiped away, and mats can be rolled or folded for easy storage. I wipe mine down with glass cleaner and a paper towel frequently to avoid transferring glue and glitter from an old project onto a new one.

Adhesives

DOUBLE-SIDED TAPE

Double-sided tape is a quick and simple adhesive that allows two sheets of paper to lie flat against each other. There's no wait time for this adhesive to dry, allowing you to continue your crafting right away!

FOAM MOUNTING TAPE

Foam mounting tape allows you to adhere two pieces of paper while adding dimension to a project. It comes in various widths and depths to suit your specific project needs. Like double-sided tape, there is no need to wait for this adhesive to dry.

GLUE PEN

A glue pen allows for spare, thin-line glue application. It is helpful when navigating tight spaces and delicate shapes and cutouts.

GLUE STICK

Standard glue sticks are perfect for many paper-cutting projects. They deposit just the right amount of glue to adhere paper, without drips. Make sure to pick a clear-drying variety to avoid residues on your finished project.

HOT GLUE GUN

This inexpensive tool should be in every crafter's gadget drawer. A strong and permanent adhesive, hot glue is easy to work with and dries quickly.

LOW-TACK TAPE

Low-tack tape can be gently repositioned or removed, allowing you to make slight adjustments on your card until you are completely happy with the placement of an element. This adhesive is great to use for projects-in-progress, but is rarely used in a final project, as it is not considered a permanent adhesive.

TACKY GLUE

Tacky glue sets very quickly. When compared to standard white glue, tacky glue is just as easy to find on store shelves, and its slightly thicker formula makes it much easier to work with.

TRANSPARENT CELLULOSE TAPE

Perfect for permanently joining paper together, transparent cellulose tape is strong and clear. This easy-tear adhesive is available in many colors, but for paper crafts the transparent variety is the most versatile.

Other Supplies of Note

45° TRIANGLE OR T-SQUARE

You might have used this tool in school and forgotten all about it, but as an adult crafter you'll soon realize how helpful it is. Place it atop a ruler and you can now draw a perfectly perpendicular (90°) line or a 45° angle.

DECOUPAGE MEDIUM

A dual-purpose adhesive and sealant, decoupage medium is a wonderful craft-drawer staple. Many projects in this book utilize decoupage medium to seal applied glitter. This prevents the glitter from flaking off the project, preserving the look of your item, and preventing a season-long mess. I call sealed glitter "polite glitter." Decoupage medium comes in many varieties, the projects in this book will work well with the gloss finish.

GLITTER

Glitter comes in different sizes. Unless otherwise specified, standard glitter is effective for the projects in this book. In special cases, coarse glitter and tinsel glitter can add different effects to your crafts.

WASHI TAPE

This paper tape comes in a wide array of colors and patterns. While not a strong adhesive, washi tape is a fabulous design element. It can be easily repositioned and creates neat and colorful edges or borders.

Scherenschnitte (Paper Cutting) Basics

Scherenschnitte isn't as difficult as it looks, but it does require great care and a good amount of pressure. Whether you're working with a printed template placed on top of cardstock or a design drawn directly onto your cardstock, you're going to want to follow some simple rules:

- Work with a very sharp craft knife, as it will slice more easily through the paper and won't pull or snag.

- Work on a self-healing cutting mat. Your blade will last longer, and printed measurement lines help cuts to stay precise and straight.

- Cut away from your torso. Cutting toward your own hand, chest, or lap puts you at much greater risk for injury.

- Cut along lines in one fluid motion. Don't stop until you reach a corner or point. Starting and stopping in the middle of the line will cause little bits of unevenness that are difficult to correct.

- Always use paper that is colored all the way through. White paper with a thin colored coating looks sloppy, and any imperfections in your cuts will be made even more apparent by the pop of white paper core.

Working with Templates

A classic transferring tool, tracing paper is easy to find and very affordable. Lay a sheet of tracing paper over your desired template and use a pencil to trace along the lines of the template. Arrange the tracing paper on top of your cardstock and secure with low-tack tape, then cut through both the tracing paper and cardstock simultaneously.

For templates that need to be resized, photocopy the template at the specified percentage. You can then secure your enlarged or reduced copy to cardstock with low-tack tape as you would with tracing paper.

MERRY
+
BRIGHT

wrapped with joy
gift toppers & greeting cards

Materials & Tools

Tracing paper

Pencil

3 sheets 12″ × 12″ red cardstock

Scissors

Bone folder

Small paint brush

White glue

Red glitter

Decoupage medium

Self-healing cutting mat

Craft knife

4 small yellow brads

Low-tack tape

Poinsettia
GIFT TOPPER

designed by **ANASTASIA BOSAKOWSKI**

This gift topper is a seasonal stand-in for bows! You can always size the templates up or down with a scanner or printer to fit larger or smaller gifts.

Instructions

1 / Using tracing paper and a pencil, copy the four poinsetta templates (see page 118) onto the cardstock, and cut out the shapes.

2 / With a bone folder, make a crease down the center of each petal, stopping before you've reached the center of the flower.

TIP

For an especially eye-catching gift, add glitter to the poinsettia. Working with a small paint brush in small sections, paint the edge of each petal and the creases with a thin amount of white glue. Sprinkle on red glitter, and tap off the excess. Allow to dry. Seal all the glitter with a small amount of decoupage medium. Allow to dry.

3 / On a self-healing cutting mat, arrange the four pieces by stacking them on top of each other in size order, with the largest at the bottom (see photo). Ensure that the petals from each cutout piece align between the petals of the one above.

4 / Once the flower petals are arranged to your liking, use a craft knife to pierce four holes through the center of the flower, arranging them in the shape of a square or diamond. Make sure to pierce through all four layers of the petals (Figure 1).

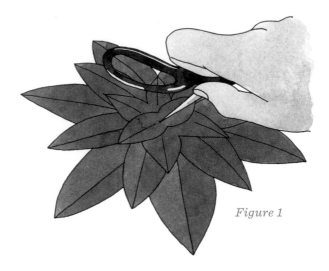

Figure 1

5 / Carefully holding the petals in place, lift the flower up off the cutting mat, and push one brad through each of the four holes. Open the backs of the brads to secure them.

6 / Attach this poinsettia to packages with low-tack tape so your recipient can reuse it as holiday decor.

Materials & Tools

1 old hardcover book (you'll need fewer than 25 pages)

Tracing paper

Pencil

Scissors

Guillotine cutter (optional)

4 sheets 8½" × 11" red printer paper

Cellophane tape

One empty cereal box (or similar cardboard)

Hot glue gun

Hot glue sticks

1 sheet 12" × 12" red cardstock

Chopstick or pencil that is smoothly round

Double-sided tape or packing tape (optional)

TIP *A word of warning: Consider the story on the pages of the book. You wouldn't want to accidentally give someone a gift with unkind or unsavory words written on it!*

Old Book
GIFT TOPPER

designed by ANASTASIA BOSAKOWSKI

Not every book is going to be reread. Why not repurpose forgotten books into pretty gift toppers or wreaths (see page 71)? If you don't have old books to use, you can always grab some at garage sales or thrift shops. Try more than one topper at once. You'll find that they come together quickly and are useful to have on hand for gift wrapping year round.

Instructions

1 / Tear out about 25 of pages from the book. Use tracing paper and pencil, transfer 20 large squares and 15 of the smallest squares from book gift topper template (see page 119). Using scissors, or, ideally, a guillotine cutter (if available), cut out the shapes from the book pages.

2 / Do the same using the red printer paper. Make about 16 squares of the medium size from the template (see page 119).

3 / Roll each square into a cone, and use a bit of tape to hold it. You'll want to make these cones as uniform as possible (**Figure 1**). You should now have 35 book page cones and 16 red paper cones.

4 / Use the provided book gift topper template (see page 119) to copy a circle onto the cardboard. Cut out the shape. Be sure to transfer the inner circle and the centerpoint guidelines onto the cardboard, but cut around the outermost circle only.

5 / Heat up your hot glue gun. Working with the largest cones from the 3" squares of paper, imagine the circle is the face of a clock. Glue a cone where the 12, 3, 6, and 9 on the clockface would be. Secure the tip of each cone along the outermost edge of the circle, allowing the rest of each cone to hang off the edges of the cardboard base (**Figure 2**). After you have those first four cones in place, fill in the space between them with additional cones, making sure they are tightly packed without squeezing neighboring cones out of shape.

Figure 1

Figure 2

6 / Repeat step 5 with the red cones, this time lining up the tip of each cone around the inner circle that you transferred in step 4 (**Figure 3**). Draw a line of glue across the back of the cone from tip to trumpet end, then rest it atop the cardboard and the previous layer of cones.

7 / Using the smallest cones from the 2" × 2" squares of paper, repeat step 5. This time line the tips of the cones up with the center dot.

8 / Using the provided template (see page 119), copy about 25 strips onto red cardstock. Cut out the shapes. Tightly wrap each strip around a chopstick or pencil, hold for a few seconds, then release. The strip of paper should now be tightly coiled.

9 / Glue three of the coils to the center of the gift topper, crossing the strips to form a six-pointed star. Glue the rest of the coils into the center of the gift topper, filling in any extra space.

TIP

You can gently bend each coiled strip up to allow it to rest along with the slope of the book pages surrounding it.

10 / Use double-sided tape, hot glue, or a thick loop of packing tape to attach the topper to a gift.

TIP

Try cutting some of the coiled strips in half to better fill every gap of space.

Figure 3

Materials & Tools

Pencil

Tracing paper

Craft knife

Self-healing cutting mat

Ruler

Cellophane tape

Double-sided tape

For the Be Merry Card

1 brown foldover card
(A2 size: 4.25" × 5.5")

1 white foldover card
(A2 size: 4.25" × 5.5")

1 sheet green paper

For the Be Merry + Bright Card

1 brown foldover card
(A2 size: 4.25" × 5.5")

1 red foldover card
(A2 size: 4.25" × 5.5")

For the Ornament Card

1 brown flat card
(A2 size: 4.25" × 5.5")

1 red foldover card
(A2 size: 4.25" × 5.5")

Festive Trio

CARDS

designed by ALEXANDRA HARRISON

These festive cards are quick and simple to make—the perfect handmade items for large groups of friends and family!

Be Merry Card Instructions

1 / Using a pencil and tracing paper, transfer the speech bubble template (see page 120) onto the inside front flap of the brown card. Take care to ensure that the lettering within the speech bubble is printed backward and that each letter is connected to the line above it.

2 / Place the card onto a self-healing cutting mat, and using a craft knife, begin to cut around the template. Start with the delicate lettering, making sure that each letter within the speech bubble is left connected to the card— don't cut the letters free! Then work your way around the rest of the design.

3 / Once you've cut out the whole design, measure the speech bubble with the ruler, and cut out a piece of green paper that is a little larger than the bubble.

4 / Tape the green paper to the inside of the brown card, behind the speech bubble. From the front of the card, the speech bubble should be the only cutout that appears green.

5 / Place double-sided tape onto the four inside corners of the brown card.

6 / Press the white foldover card inside the brown card. Carefully line up the corners, and press down to ensure neat placement.

Ornament Card Instructions

1 / Using a pencil and tracing paper, transfer the ornament template (see page 120) onto the brown card.

2 / With the brown card on a cutting mat, carefully cut along the lines of the template with a craft knife.

3 / Place double-sided tape onto back side of the brown card, pressing tape into each corner and within the ornaments.

4 / Press the brown card onto the front flap of the red foldover card. Line up the corners, and then press down to ensure neat placement.

Merry + Bright Card Instructions

1 / Using a pencil and tracing paper, transfer the MERRY + BRIGHT template (see page 120) onto the brown card. Take care to ensure that the lettering is printed backward.

2 / With the brown card on the cutting mat, begin to cut around the template with a craft knife. Start with the delicate lettering, and move on to the wreath pattern. Make sure that each leaf is separate and detached from the curved line of the wreath.

3 / Place double-sided tape onto the back side of the brown card, pressing the tape into each corner, beside the letters and within the wreath.

4 / Press the brown card onto the front flap of the red foldover card. Line up the corners, and then press down to ensure neat placement.

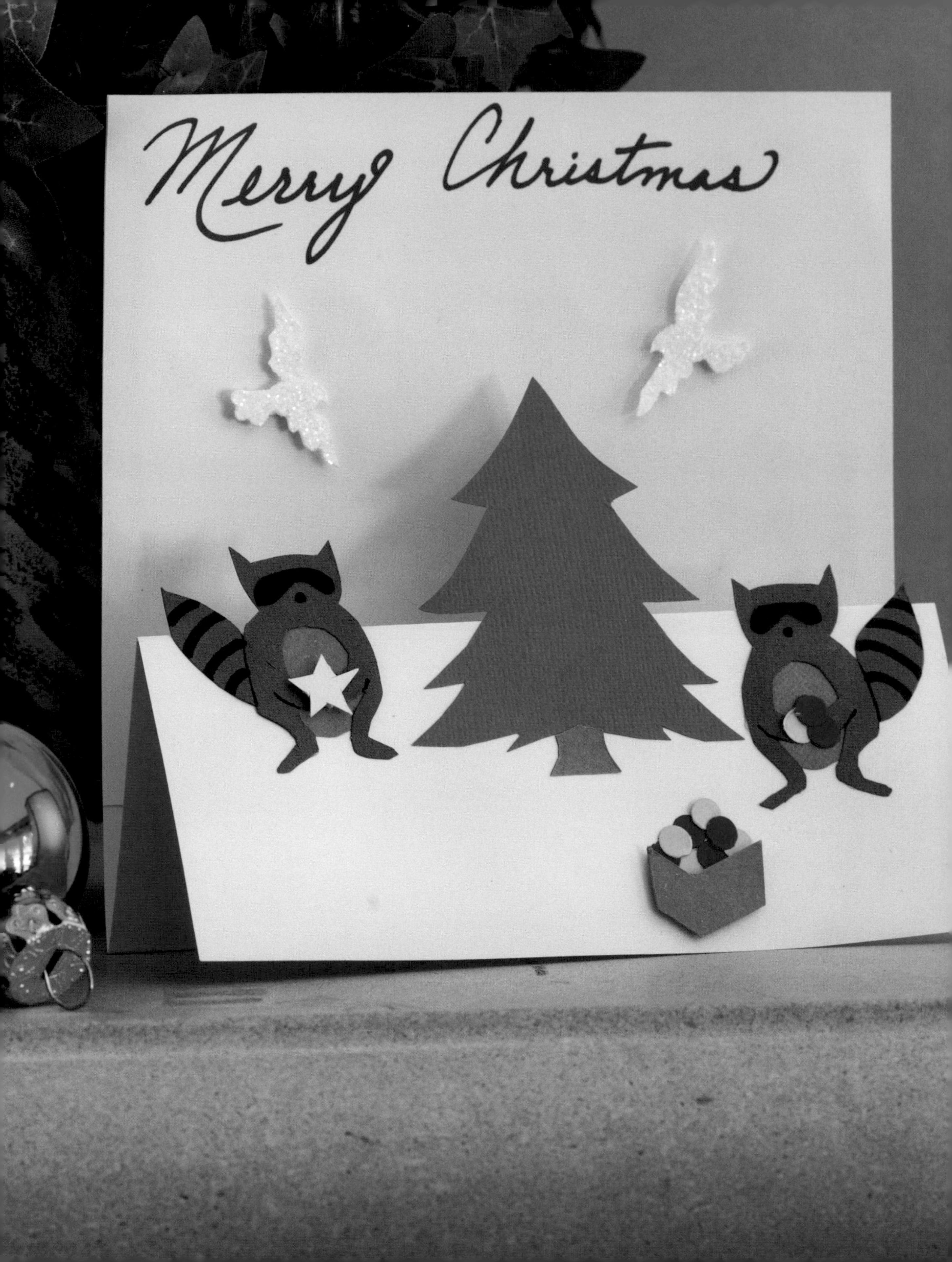
Merry Christmas

Materials & Tools

Scissors

Ruler

1 sheet 12″ × 12″ light blue cardstock

Bone folder

Thick-point red marker

Pencil (optional)

Craft knife

Self-healing cutting mat

1 sheet 12″ × 12″ green cardstock

1 sheet 12″ × 12″ gray cardstock

1 sheet 12″ × 12″ brown cardstock

1 sheet 12″ × 12″ white cardstock

Scraps of black, red, and yellow cardstock

¼″ hole punch

Small paint brush

Tacky glue

Coarse white glitter

Gloss decoupage medium

Fine-point black marker

Thick-point black marker

Foam mounting tape

Raccoon
CARD

designed by ANASTASIA BOSAKOWSKI

Lots of people rig up ways to display their Christmas cards. Why not make it easy for them by creating a card that was born to stand on its own? You can write your holiday greeting on a cleverly hidden fold-back panel or write it on the back of the card.

Instructions

1 / Cut the light blue cardstock to 6" × 11". Laying the paper vertically in front of you (with a 6" edge closest to you), score a horizontal line 2½" from the bottom edge of the cardstock. Unfold and flip the card over. Measure 5" from the bottom edge of the paper (2½" up from the first fold), and score another line. The folds should face in opposite directions, creating a zigzag in the cardstock (**Figure 1**).

2 / Using a red marker, write *Merry Christmas* across the top of the card. Set aside.

> **TIP**
>
> *It is a good idea to plan out your lettering in pencil before writing your message in marker. If you are unhappy with the lettering, you will need to cut a new card blank and begin again!*

3 / With a craft knife and cutting mat, and using the provided raccoon templates (see page 121), cut out the tree from green cardstock and the raccoon bodies from gray cardstock. Cut the raccoon bellies, tree stump, and crate from brown cardstock and the doves from white cardstock. Cut the raccoons' eye masks from black cardstock and the star from yellow cardstock. Use the hole punch to cut out six circles each from red and yellow cardstock. Set all cutouts aside.

4 / Using a small paint brush, coat each of the doves with a thin layer of tacky glue. Sprinkle coarse white glitter over the glue, tap off the excess, and allow to dry. Once dry, paint a thin layer of decoupage medium over the glitter. Set aside to dry.

5 / Position the raccoons' brown bellies over their gray bodies, and glue into place. Using a thin black marker, draw lines for the arms, using project photo to the left as a guide. Use a thick black marker to make the stripes on the tails and dots for the noses. Position the black masks over the raccoons' faces, and glue into place. Use the punched circles to arrange a bouquet of "ornaments" into the arms of one

> **TIP**
>
> *For a dramatic, extra-thick layer of glitter, paint a thin coat of decoupage medium on top of the first coating of glitter. Sprinkle on another layer of white glitter, and allow to dry. Finish with another thin coat of decoupage medium.*

raccoon, and glue into place. Use foam mounting tape to secure the star between the arms of the other raccoon.

6 / Using the project photo to the right as a guide, arrange the tree and raccoons on the 2½" front fold of the card, being sure that the tree and raccoon heads stick up above the fold. Paint a thin layer of glue onto the back of the tree stump, tree, and raccoons, and secure into place.

7 / Use foam mounting tape to secure the crate and doves into place. Glue a few extra hole-punched "ornaments" into the crate.

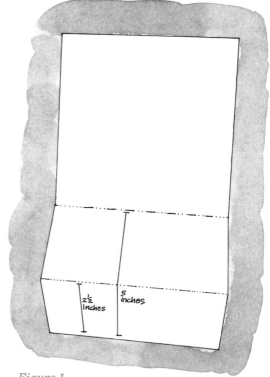

Figure 1

gathering around the table
decor for mantelpieces & tables

Materials & Tools

2 sheets 8½″ × 11″ printer paper

Carbon paper

1 sheet 8½″ × 11″ cream-colored cardstock (or color of your choice)

Pencil

Craft knife

Self-healing cutting mat

Box frame with depth of at least 1″

Ruler

Scissors

Paint brush, medium to large size

Dark blue acrylic paint (or color of your choice)

Paper glue or super glue

Paper Stag
SHADOWBOX

designed by SILVINA DE VITA

This shadowbox can be a special gift or a decoration for your own home. Inspired by the woods in Richmond Park, London, this night scene will give you the opportunity to show off your talents to your guests this Christmas.

Instructions

1 / Draw or print the paper stag templates (see page 122) onto a sheet of printer paper.

2 / Place the carbon paper on top of the cardstock, and then place the printer paper pattern on top of the carbon paper.

3 / Using a pencil, trace over each element on the printer paper, using firm and steady pressure. This will transfer the pictures onto the cardstock. You can put as much or as little detail around the edges as you want.

4 / Using a craft knife and cutting mat, cut around each image on the cardstock.

5 / Measure the back panel of the shadowbox. Transfer a rectangle of the same dimensions to the second sheet of printer paper, and cut along the lines. This will be the backdrop to the shadowbox. Using a medium-to-large-sized paint brush, completely paint the backdrop with acrylic paint in the color of your choice. (I used dark blue.)

TIP

The background for the shadowbox can be any pattern or color, as long as it fits in the box. You can explore texture with specialty paper, patterns with wrapping or scrapbook paper, or pictures for a scenic background.

6 / Using paper glue, affix the backdrop inside the back of the shadowbox and the moon to the backdrop.

7 / Before you glue the trees to the box, place the stag at the front of the box.

8 / The stag and tree cutouts each have a small base that will need to be folded backward at 90°. This forms a base for the figure. Fold up each base, then arrange the pieces in the box until you are happy with their placement.

9 / Glue along the base of the stag, and affix it to the inner bottom edge of the box.

10 / Glue the trees inside the box.

11 / Close and secure the shadowbox, and enjoy your lovely night scene.

Materials & Tools

Pencil

1 sheet 8½″ × 11″ printer paper

Carbon paper

2 sheets 8½″ × 11″ cream cardstock (or color of your choice)

Craft knife

Self-healing cutting mat

Paper glue

Glass dome with wooden base, approximately 1′ in height (can be found online or in any antique shop)

Super glue (optional)

Welcome Home
GLASS DOME

designed by SILVINA DE VITA

Inspired by fairy tales, this little paper house is a unique creation to display with pride in your home. Especially festive at Christmastime, it can be enjoyed all year round.

Instructions

1 / Draw or photocopy welcome home templates (see page 123) onto a sheet of printer paper.

2 / Place the carbon paper on top of the cardstock, and then place the printer paper on top of the carbon paper.

3 / With a pencil, trace over the house, trees, leaves, and gate, using firm and steady pressure. This will transfer the pictures onto the card beneath. You can put as much or as little detail around the edges as you want.

4 / Use a craft knife and cutting mat to cut out the transferred images.

5 / Glue the house cutout into the center of the dome. Allow glue to dry.

6 / Working with both tree cutouts and the gate cutout, form a circle (use the project photo as a guide). Glue these cutouts together, and allow to dry.

7 / Glue the trees and gate onto dome base, ensuring that house is centered inside the circle.

8 / Glue the leaves on the trees. Use as many leaves as you would like to modify the feeling of the dome. For a sparse, winter scene, use fewer leaves. For a lush, summery scene, use an abundance of leaves.

9 / Glue the bike at the back of the house, or anywhere you like.

10 / Lower the glass dome over the base.

> **TIP**
>
> *For extra security, you can attach the dome to its base using super glue.*

Materials & Tools

Pencil

1 sheet 12″ × 12″ dark green cardstock

2 sheets 12″ × 12″ white cardstock

Small, very sharp scissors

Craft knife

Self-healing cutting mat

White craft paint

Paint mixing dish or disposable plate

Coarse white glitter

Small paint brush

Hole punch

Ribbon or string

Low-tack tape (optional)

1 sheet Indigo cardstock (optional)

Tacky glue (optional)

Decoupage medium (optional)

Wolf, Polar Bear & Tree
SILHOUETTES

designed by ANASTASIA BOSAKOWSKI

These silhouettes are simple to make but ever so striking. They look fantastic when placed on a bookshelf to bring winter's chill to your reading materials. You can shrink them down to use on greeting cards, or set them against a sea of cut snowflakes for a beautiful window display.

Instructions

1 / Carefully transfer the tree template (see page 124) onto green cardstock. Cut out the tree.

2 / Carefully transfer the wolf and bear templates (see page 124) onto white cardstock.

TIP

Align the bottom edges of the templates with the bottom of the sheet of cardstock to result in perfectly level, straight bottom edges for the cutouts.

3 / Cut out the wolf and the bear. You can use either small, very sharp scissors or a craft knife to cut out the silhouettes. Scissors can be useful for the longer cuts, while a craft knife and cutting mat is helpful for all of the highly detailed bits. When using a craft knife, use firm pressure, cut away from yourself, and cut in one fluid stroke from one corner or point to the next. Set the cutouts aside.

4 / Squeeze a mound of white paint about the size of a quarter onto a paint mixing dish or disposable plate. By eye, pour roughly the same amount of glitter into the paint, and stir with the paint brush. It might seem like there's too much glitter at first, but you'll soon have a thick, grainy paint that will make a dimensional snow that you can paint onto the tree.

TIP

These silhouettes work well for cardmaking! Simply fold a sheet of indigo cardstock, and glue on the silhouette of your choice using tacky glue. Now, use the textured snow paint from step 3 to add a setting around the wolf, bear, or tree! Make sure to paint over any dimensional paint with decoupage medium to seal and protect the card.

5 / Using the photo at right as a guide, paint snow onto the tree. Dab the paint on, don't brush it, to get a nice, raised texture. Follow the curves of the tree's branches to create a natural look. Set it aside to dry.

6 / Use a hole punch and ribbon or string to hang the cutouts as ornaments . Or apply low-tack tape, adhere and tape to a window to create beautiful window silhouettes. They even look great leaning up against bookshelves!

Materials & Tools

Pencil

Ruler

6 sheets 12″ × 12″ scrapbook paper

Scissors

Glue pen

Hot glue gun

Hot glue sticks

3D Tree
CENTERPIECE

designed by **ANASTASIA BOSAKOWSKI**

This tree looks beautiful on a mantle or side table. Make multiple trees for a beautiful forest centerpiece! This tree is constructed in much the same way as the Polish Star (page 103), so after you've completed this project, try your hand at the Polish Star for beautiful matching decor!

Instructions

1 / Using a pencil and ruler, transfer all seven 3D tree templates (see page 125) to the wrong side of the scrapbook paper. Make sure to transfer the dotted inner guidelines.

2 / Using scissors, cut out all seven template shapes. Cut along the indicated spokes.

3 / Gently fold each "petal" in half, creating a crease (Figure 1).

4 / Continuing to work on the back of the paper (patterned-side down), place the tip of a pencil into the crease at the edge of a petal. Roll the paper around the tip of the pencil, creating a cone. Roll the left side in, then draw a thin line of glue along the edge of the right side and roll in to meet the left corner. Hold in place for about 5 seconds to secure (Figure 2).

5 / Continue to create a cone for each "petal" until all 11 points are complete (Figure 3).

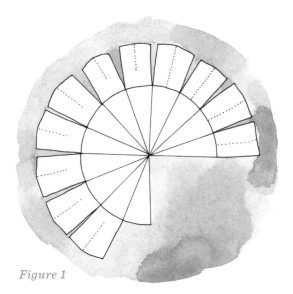

Figure 1

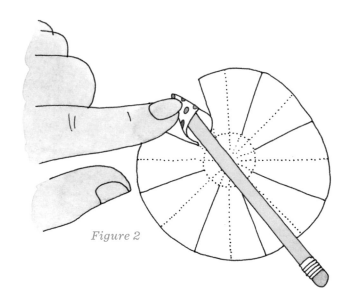

Figure 2

6 / Gently bring both sides of the open wedge together. Apply a thin layer of glue to the final wedge on the templated shape. Bring this wedge across the open wedge, gently curving the cut paper. Secure the cutout into this closed position (**Figure 4**).

7 / Repeat steps 3 through 6 for all seven tiers of the tree.

8 / Arrange the cones in order from template A (smallest) to template G (largest). Carefully stack each tier, with template F on the bottom, and template A on top. Arrange each level so that its points sit between the points of the tier below it. Once you're pleased with the alignment of each tier, lift cutout A and generously apply dots of hot glue to the tier under it (B). Press tier A back into place, and hold it in position for a few moments to allow the glue to set. Repeat this process with all of the tiers, until each tier of the tree has been secured.

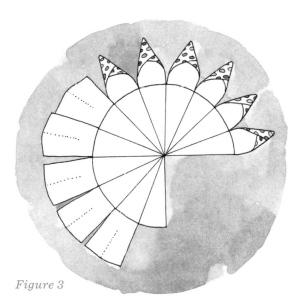

Figure 3

Figure 4

Materials & Tools

Pencil

2 sheets tracing paper

2 sheets 12″ × 12″ light blue cardstock

Craft knife

Self-healing cutting mat

Scissors

Bone folder

2 sheets 8½″ × 11″ vellum

Ruler (optional)

Guillotine cutter (optional)

Scrap cardstock

Tacky glue

1 roll ½″ washi tape in a design of your choosing

4-pack of LED color-changing tea lights

TIP *Make sure to use electric tea lights (color-changing LED lights are a festive option). Using real candles with paper crafts can lead to disaster.*

Noel
LUMINARIES

designed by **ANASTASIA BOSAKOWSKI**

Inspired by baby blocks, these luminaries (tea light candle covers) call out "NOEL." Be sure to display them where the sides can be seen, as they feature a leaping reindeer and jolly snowman images on alternating blocks.

Instructions

1 / Using a pencil and tracing paper, transfer the four luminaries templates (see pages 126–127) onto the back of the blue cardstock. Ensure that the letters on each template are backward.

2 / Using a craft knife and cutting mat, cut out the inner images from each strip. Carefully press out the pieces to be removed. to avoid tearing the edges, do not force them. If you have any resistance, use the craft knife to carefully retrace your original cut.

3 / Using scissors for the long, straight edges, cut around the outer lines of each strip. Use a bone folder to score along the indicated lines. This will create a box 2" on each side with a ¼" lip for gluing. Set strips aside without gluing.

4 / Use the provided luminaries template (see pages 126–127) to cut 16 rectangles out of the vellum.

TIP

Using a ruler or a guillotine cutter to achieve nice straight edges makes cutting the vellum rectangles a snap.

5 / Using a piece of scrap cardstock, very carefully spread a thin layer of tacky glue on the inside of the luminary. Don't get too close to the edges of the design, since you don't want glue to ooze out of the holes. Press one rectangle of vellum onto the back of each panel of the luminaries. Take care to avoid getting vellum into the folds, as this will prevent the luminary from folding properly. Repeat until all panels are covered with vellum. Allow to dry.

6 / Flip each strip over to allow the outer side of the luminary to face up. Apply a strip of washi tape along the entire bottom of the strip. Trim off the excess with your craft knife. Repeat along the top. Apply washi tape to each luminary.

7 / Fold along the scored folds from step 3. Apply tacky glue to the outside of the ¼" lip, and press it onto the inside of the luminary.

8 / If you have difficulty securing the luminary into its three-dimensional shape, use the bone folder to press the inner lip into place.

9 / Once the glue is set, stand each luminary up around a switched-on LED tea light for a festive display!

Materials & Tools

Foam brush

1 Styrofoam egg ($2^5/_{16}"$ × $3^1/_{16}"$)

Brown craft paint

Pencil

Tracing paper

Scissors (small)

3" × 3" piece of cardboard (an old cereal box is perfect)

4 sheets 12" × 12" brown cardstock

Craft knife

Self-healing cutting mat

White craft paint

Disposable plate (Styrofoam or paper)

Coarse white glitter

Small paint brush

Decoupage medium

Silver glitter

Hot glue gun

Hot glue sticks

3 pennies

Bottle cap from 2-liter soda bottle

Washi tape

1 piece 3" × 3" of white cardstock

Fine-point black marker

Red glitter

$1/_4"$ double-sided tape

Pinecone
PLACE CARD HOLDER

designed by **ANASTASIA BOSAKOWSKI**

These pinecones take a bit of time, but boy, are they impressive! I find that you can easily cut out all of the little pieces while watching television. Then, once you have a pile of them, sit down and make a few pinecones in couple of hours. You can reuse this project year after year (if you can keep guests from taking them home)!

Instructions

1 / Using a foam brush, cover the Styrofoam egg in brown paint. Set aside to dry.

2 / Using a pencil, trace both pinecone templates (see page 127) onto tracing paper. Using scissors, cut out the shapes from the tracing paper, then trace around them onto the cardboard. Cut out the cardboard shapes: These are your stencils. Trace the large cardboard teardrop onto brown cardstock. Repeat until you have 90 large teardrops. Repeat 40 times with the smaller template. You might want to create a few spares so you don't get caught short at the end.

3 / Using a craft knife and cutting mat or scissors, cut out all of the teardrop shapes from the brown cardstock.

4 / Wind each teardrop cutout around a pencil to give it a gentle curve. Hold the pointed end of the teardrop against the pencil's shaft, and roll upward (**Figure 1**).

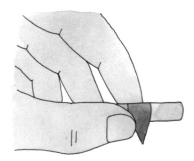

Figure 1

5 / Dispense a quarter-sized mound of white paint onto a disposable plate. Pour an equal amount of coarse white glitter into the paint, and stir with a small paint brush. It might seem too thick at first, but the mixture will incorporate. Use this mixture to paint little arcs along the tips of all the teardrops to give a snow effect. Allow to dry.

6 / When all of the paint has dried, use decoupage medium to paint over the glitter paint on each teardrop, and sprinkle the wet coating with silver glitter. Allow to dry.

7 / Heat up your hot glue gun. You will begin by working with the smaller teardrops to cover the narrow tip of the egg. Place a dot of glue onto to the point of each teardrop, and press onto the egg (**Figure 2**). Work in a circle, ensuring that the teardrops overlap and the Styrofoam does not show through. Don't worry about lining up each teardrop perfectly—after all, nature isn't so orderly.

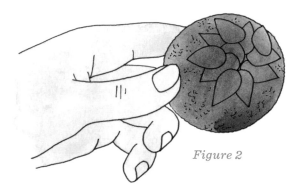

Figure 2

TIP

When working with a hot glue gun, lots of gossamer strings of glue will form and get caught in your work. You'll be tempted to stop what you're doing to remove them—don't ! Finish all of your work, and then wait about 2 minutes. Now you can pull off all of the strings. They'll be cool and dry, so they won't keep finding new things to stick to and will be easier to peel away.

8 / When you have completed a full circle of teardrops, begin working your way down the egg in overlapping rounds. Place the next row of teardrops approximately ¼" below the first, ensuring that all Styrofoam is covered (**Figure 3**).

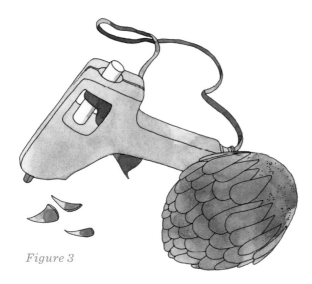

Figure 3

9 / When you have completed three rounds of small teardrops, begin working with the larger cutouts. Continue to work in overlapping rounds. When you reach the curved base of the egg, switch back to the smaller teardrops to finish covering the egg. Once the egg is covered, set it aside to dry.

10 / Glue the pennies into the bottle cap. Begin by squeezing a drop of hot glue into the bottom of the cap, and pressing the first penny into the drop of glue. Squeeze another dot of hot glue onto the penny, and top with a second coin. Repeat for all 3 pennies, sandwiching each with a dot of hot glue. When all three coins are secured, fill in the cap with more glue, covering and surrounding the pennies but ensuring that the cap does not overflow. Allow to dry. Wrap the outer edge of the bottle cap in washi tape. If the washi tape is too wide for the cap, you can trim the edges, or fold them under the bottom of the bottle cap. Carefully squeeze a large mound of hot glue into the bottle cap,

ensuring that it reaches just above the lid's rim. Carefully settle the egg into the glue, making sure it's well centered. Allow to dry.

11 / Use the provided template (see page 127) to trace the banner shape onto white cardstock. Cut out the banner. Using a fine-tipped marker, carefully write your guest's name onto the banner, making sure to leave approximately ¼" of space on each end of the banner. Carefully paint a thin layer of decoupage medium onto both ends of the banner. Sprinkle with red glitter, and tap off any excess. Allow to dry. For perfectly straight lines on the name banner, use double-sided tape to affix the red glitter instead of decoupage medium.

12 / Using a strip of double-sided tape, affix the name banner onto the pinecone. Stunning!

TIP

For a clean and professional finish, and to prevent glitter from littering your dinner table, paint over the red glitter on the banner with a thin coating of decoupage medium. This will seal the glitter in and help to prevent a glittery mess!

Materials & Tools

3 sheets 8½″ × 11″ printer paper

Glue stick

Scissors

Craft knife (optional)

Self-healing cutting mat (optional)

3D Paper Reindeer
CENTERPIECE

designed by ELLEN DEAKIN

Get crafty with these gorgeous paper reindeers! Create a fantastic festive centerpiece or mantelpiece decoration with this colorful trio of holiday friends.

Instructions

1 / Photocopy the 3D reindeer templates (see pages 128–130) onto 8½" × 11" printer paper.

2 / Fold the template as indicated on pages 128–130 so that the reindeer pattern and the solid panel are back-to-back, and then glue together

3 / Using either scissors or a craft knife and cutting mat, cut out the pieces of the reindeer. Cut slits where indicated by a white line.

4 / Attach the ears, antlers, and tail to the body of the reindeer. Next, attach the legs to the oval disks, and then attach the disks to the body.

Materials & Tools

Pencil

7 sheets 12″ × 12″ scrapbook paper in 2 green patterns

Scissors

1 sheet 12″ × 12″ red cardstock

Small paint brush

Tacky glue

Gold glitter

Decoupage medium

Trifold presentation board, 36″ × 48″ white corrugated cardboard

18″ ruler

Self-healing cutting mat

Craft knife

Light green craft paint

1″ foam brush

Glue pen

¼″ hole punch

25 bite-sized chocolates

Red and white baker's twine

25 red brads (I painted brass brads red)

Hot glue gun

Hot glue sticks

8″ store-bought gold bow or Finnish star (see page 95)

1 sheet 12″ × 12″ white cardstock

1 sheet 12″ × 12″ yellow cardstock

Snowflake punch

Advent
CALENDAR

designed by **ANASTASIA BOSAKOWSKI**

I didn't have an advent calendar until I was an adult living in England. When I was introduced to the idea, I thought it was fantastic—stretch out the excitement of the Christmas season with a piece of chocolate every day? Yes, please! These envelopes will fit a little fun-sized chocolate bar, but you could slip in love notes or coupons for a hug, a kiss, or an even bigger bar of chocolate! This project seems a bit involved at first glimpse, but it can easily be made in a weekend.

Instructions

1 / Use the provided advent calendar template (see page 131) to transfer 25 envelope shapes onto green cardstock. Using scissors, cut out. Fold along indicated dotted lines.

TIP

Decorative scissors create a beautiful edge for the flap of the envelope.

2 / Using the provided advent calendar template (see page 131), cut out 25 circles from the red cardstock. Use a pencil to sketch numbers 1 through 25 on each circle. Make sure to align the numbers within the bottom half of the red circle to prevent them from being obscured by the envelope's flap. When you are happy with their alignment, paint over the numbers with tacky glue. Dust with gold glitter, and tap off the excess. When the glue is dry, paint a thin coating of decoupage medium over the glitter, and set aside to dry.

3 / While the circles are drying, build the tree. Start with a trifold presentation board (you can buy these at office supply stores). Cut off the two side panels. Holding the board vertically cut off an additional 3" of the width. Draw a dot along the center of the board's top edge, and draw diagonal lines from that dot to the bottom corners to form the triangular tree. Cut along those lines. You'll get the neatest cut by placing the board on a cutting mat, holding a ruler along the line as a guide, and slicing through the board with a craft knife. Do not dispose of the pieces you've cut from the board.

4 / Paint the board light green with a foam brush, and set aside to dry.

5 / While the presentation board dries, attach one red circle to each of the envelopes with glue pen. Carefully position each circle below the envelope's decorative flap (the color contrast will make the punched pattern visible).

6 / Use a hole punch to create a hole ½" below the top of each envelope. Make sure to punch through all layers of the envelope including the flap.

7 / Slip one chocolate into each envelope and set aside.

8 / Measure along both sides of the tree, marking the tree 4" from the bottom edge, 8¾" from the bottom edge, 12¾" from the bottom edge, 17½" from the bottom edge, 21½" from the bottom edge, and 25½" from the bottom edge. At each marking, cut a notch about ⅜" deep into the edge of the cardboard. These notches will hold each string of hanging envelopes. Cut the notches at a very subtle downward angle to help the envelopes stay in place.

9 / Cut seven lengths of baker's twine measuring approximately 3 feet each. These will be trimmed later, so do not worry about achieving an exact measurement.

10 / Lay the cardboard tree on a work surface, and loosely drape each length of twine across the tree, lining each length of twine up with the notches you cut in step 8.

11 / Carefully plan the placement of the 25 envelopes along each length of twine on the tree. When you are happy with the arrangement of the envelopes, slip the flap of the envelope over the appropriate length of twine, allowing the envelope to close over the twine. Secure the envelope by placing a brad through the envelope's punched hole, and opening the tabs to secure. The brad should rest below the twine.

12 / You should now have 25 envelopes secured onto seven lengths of twine. Secure each length of twine by sliding its ends into the slits on either side of the tree. Carefully pull the twine to your desired tightness, and tie a double knot at the back of the tree to secure. Trim any extra twine.

> *Be sure to tighten each strand enough to prevent any envelopes from overlapping.*

13 / Make the stand: Take one triangle of cardboard you removed in step 6. Use the provided template (see page 131) to trim the remaining cardboard into the shape of the stand. Fold where indicated. Apply glue along the folded flap and adhere to the center of the tree to form a stand (**Figure 1**). Hold in place for 30 seconds to allow a strong bond to form.

> *When gluing the stand onto the back of the tree, glue over a number of strands of twine. This will help to hold the twine in place.*

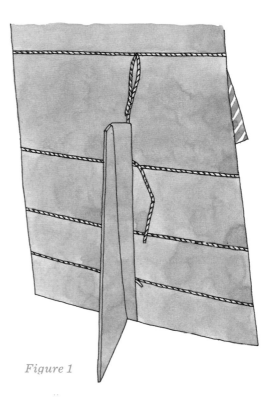

Figure 1

14 / Using a snowflake punch, create 10–15 snowflakes out of white cardstock. Repeat with yellow cardstock. Use a dot of tacky glue to secure the snowflakes across the front of the tree.

15 / Attach a store-bought gift bow or a Finnish star (see page 95) to the top, and you're ready to celebrate!

welcome to our home
wreaths & garlands

Materials & Tools

6 sheets 12″ × 12″ scrapbook paper printed on both sides

Pencil

Ruler

Scissors

Roll of double-sided tape

Stapler

Cellophane tape

Paper clip (about 2″)

TIP *This snowflake is very large (over 2½″ in diameter). You can scale the snowflake down by starting with 8″ squares.*

Snowflake

HANGING DECORATION

designed by ANASTASIA BOSAKOWSKI

Creating this snowflake feels like magic! With just six square sheets of paper, tape, and a few straight cuts, you can create an oversized, three-dimensional, conversation piece. Make one or many to wow your guests!

Instructions

1 / Take one square of paper. Fold the paper diagonally, bringing the upper left corner down to the bottom right corner. Once folded, you will have a triangle. Bring the bottom left corner of the triangle up to the upper right corner and fold.

2 / You will now have a smaller triangular shape. The bottom edge (closest to your chest) will be one solid crease. The side facing away from your chest will have two flaps, almost like rabbit ears (**Figure 1**).

3 / Using a pencil and ruler mark the following guidelines along the bottom edge: Make the first mark 2¼" from the edge, then space four more marks about ¾" apart (**Figure 2**). Using scissors, cut five straight lines from the folded edge closest to you toward the pointed edge, stopping ½" before the edge of the triangle.

4 / Unfold the paper (**Figure 3**).

5 / Take the two points from the central diamond, and stick them together with a bit of double-sided tape to create a roll (**Figure 4**).

6 / Skip the next tier of cut strips, and curl the following tier of strips in as you did in step 5. Stick the points together with double-sided tape (**Figure 5**). Be sure to line the pieces up carefully so that they look as if they are long continuous strands.

7 / Repeat step 6 until you reach the final tier of cut strips.

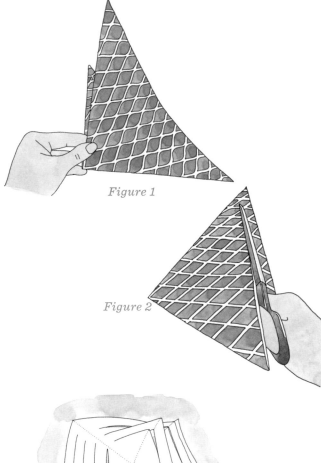

Figure 1

Figure 2

Figure 3

Figure 4

Figure 5

8 / Flip the paper over so that the curls you've just formed are face down. Starting with the two innermost flaps, repeat steps 6 and 7 (**Figure 6**).

9 / Once you've curled in all of the strips, the square should look like Figure 7.

10 / Repeat steps 1 through 9 five more times.

11 / Once you have finished taping all six shapes, lay them out on a table in a circle with their points facing in. This should resemble the final shape of the hanging snowflake. If you're using multiple patterns and colors, plan out the final arrangement of those colors now. Be sure that for each of the six pieces the center cone has been rolled in the same direction.

12 / When the arrangement is satisfactory, grasp the center-pointing tip of one of the pieces. Take the tip of the next piece over, and pinch them together so that they're lined up perfectly. Keep adding pieces until you have all six points pinched together between your fingers with the points perfectly aligned. The rest of the pieces will bunch up together (**Figure 8**).

13 / Use one staple to secure all six pieces together (**Figure 9**).

14 / Fan each piece out again to form a snowflake.

15 / Secure the outermost strip of paper on each snowflake "point" to the outermost strip of paper on the "point" next to it, by stapling the two strips together.

16 / Decide which point you would like to be the top of the snowflake. Strengthen the tip of the point by wrapping it with one layer of cellophane tape. Poke the paperclip through the paper and tape, and bend the paperclip as necessary to hang the snowflake.

Figure 8

Figure 6

Figure 9

Figure 7

Snowflake hanging decoration **69**

Materials & Tools

1 old book (you'll need 80 to 110 pages from a standard hardcover)

Guillotine cutter (optional)

Stapler

1 piece 14″ × 14″ cardboard (repurpose a mailing box or purchase a presentation board from an office supply store)

Scissors

Compass (optional)

Ruler

Hot glue gun

Hot glue sticks

1 pack of dollar-store Christmas ball ornaments

Binder clip

String or hook

Book Lover's
WREATH

designed by ANASTASIA BOSAKOWSKI

This wreath is large, impressive, and almost free to make. What's not to love? Make sure to hang it in a spot that you want to be a focal point, because it will easily draw the attention of everyone in the room!

Instructions

1 / Pull about 110 pages out from an old hardcover book. Using the provided book lover's wreath template (see page 132), trim the pages to 7" × 5½". The guillotine cutter works best for this.

2 / Take about 10 to 15 sheets at a time, and roll them from the bottom up, then side to side. This softens up the paper and makes it easier to roll.

TIP

Trimming the edges and gutters from the pages will allow you to preserve the most text per page, resulting in a neater final project.

3 / Roll each page into a cone (**Figure 1**). Secure with a staple about 1" from the point of the cone. Make about 100 cones.

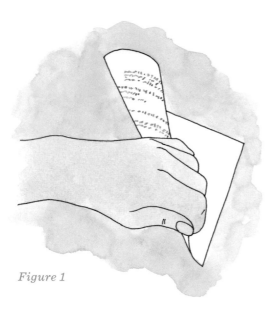

Figure 1

TIP

If you make a mark on the base of the stapler 1" from where the staples go in, you can very quickly line up each of the points with the marking and maintain a uniform position for each staple.

4 / Use the provided template (see page 133) to cut the wreath base out of cardboard. Make sure to transfer both the inner and outer circles to the cardboard. Using scissors, cut along the outer circle only.

5 / Alternatively, you can use a compass to make the cardboard wreath base. Cut the cardboard into a 14″ × 14″ square. Find the center of the square by using a ruler to draw diagonal lines between opposite corners. Using the point where the lines cross as the center, draw three concentric circles, one with an 8″ diameter, one with a 6″ diameter, and one with a 4″ diameter. Cut along the 8″ circle to create the wreath base.

6 / Heat up your glue gun. Imagine the 8" circle is the face of a clock. Glue a cone where the 12, 3, 6, and 9 would be. Align the staple on each cone with the outer edge of the wreath, allowing most of each cone to hang off of the edges of the wreath (**Figure 2**). After you have the first four cones in place, continue to glue cones around the outer edge of the wreath, nestling each cone directly next to the cone beside it.

Figure 2

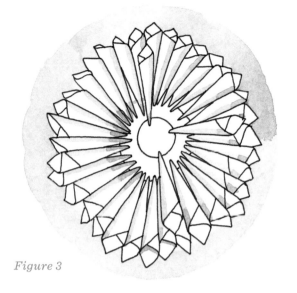

Figure 3

7 / Repeat step 5 along the middle (6") circle and the smallest (4" circle) (**Figure 3**).

8 / Create one final row of book pages.

9 / Repeat one more round, this time putting the staple for each cone on top of the center dot. (It'll get stacked a bit high.)

10 / Open up a pack of small Christmas balls. I got mine very cheaply at the dollar store—they're very lightweight, which is a plus. Glue the balls into an attractive pile in the center of the wreath as in the photo. As a nice decorative touch, add some glitter to the ornaments.

11 / Attach a binder clip to the edge of the cardboard wreath base. This can be attached to a string or a hook to hang the wreath.

Materials & Tools

3 sheets 12″ × 12″ striped scrapbook paper

Bone folder

Glue stick

Small paint brush

Decoupage medium

Silver glitter

1 sheet 12″ × 12″ yellow scrapbook paper

Craft knife

Self-healing cutting mat

Floral wire

Cellophane tape

Gold glitter

3½″ × 3½″ piece of cardboard (an old cereal box is perfect)

Scissors

Hot glue gun

Hot glue sticks

Compass

Accordion-Fold Star
DECORATION

designed by **ANASTASIA BOSAKOWSKI**

This decoration celebrates glitter and stars! A gorgeous standalone adornment, one of these stars can serve as a beautiful tree topper or as an embellishment on a gift. A grouping of three or more can fill a hallway with cheer or spice up a large undecorated wall.

Instructions

1 / For the background circle, take a striped piece of scrapbook paper, and fold it into equal sixteenths. To achieve a perfect 16-part fold, first fold the paper in half. Then fold it in half again! Repeat twice more (four total folds). Unfold for a perfect 16-segment accordion fold.

2 / Unfold the paper, and trace over each fold with a bone folder for sharp creases. Refold the paper into an accordion fold.

3 / Coat one edge of the accordion-folded strip with a glue stick and fold in half, holding in place for about 30 seconds to allow the glue to set (**Figure 1**). Allow the glue to dry.

Figure 1

TIP

For a neat finished product, make sure the folds run in the same direction as the stripes on the paper.

4 / Once the glue has dried, carefully open the accordion, creating a fan shape. Be careful not to unglue the seam you just made.

5 / Repeat steps 1 through 3 with the remaining sheets of scrapbook paper.

6 / Use a glue stick to coat the outer edges of all three fans. Join them together to create a full circle (**Figure 2**). Allow the glue to dry. It is easiest to complete this step in stages, adding glitter to four or five mountain folds at a time.

7 / With the circle face up in front of you, paint a thin stripe of decoupage medium down each of the circle's raised seams (in origami these are called the "mountain folds"). Dust with silver glitter, and tap off the excess. Once it is dry, paint over all the glitter (and only the glitter) with a thin coat of decoupage medium. Set aside to dry.

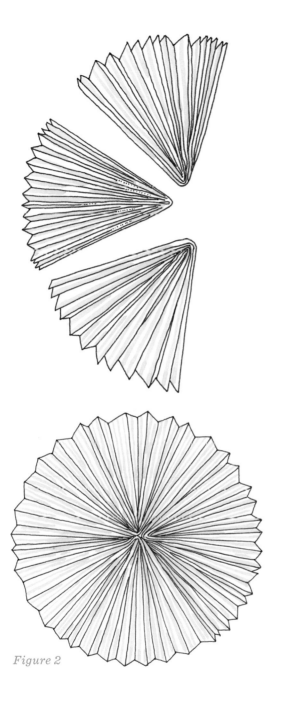

8 / For the star, take a sheet of contrasting scrapbook paper (I used yellow), and fold it into equal eighths, making sharp creases with a bone folder. To achieve a perfect 8-part fold, first fold the paper in half. Then fold it in half again. Repeat once more (three folds total). Unfold, and then refold in alternating directions for a perfect 8-segment accordion fold.

9 / Fold the accordion-folded strip in half. Ensure that the open folds are on the right side of the strip, and the closed folds are to the left.

10 / Line up the provided star wall hanging template (see page 134) on top of the accordion-folded strip. Using a craft knife and cutting mat, cut through all layers of paper, creating a long triangle with a cutout notch.

11 / Fold a 12" piece of floral wire in half. Wrap the wire around the center fold of the accordion-folded strip, and twist the two loose ends together to secure the star (Figure 3).

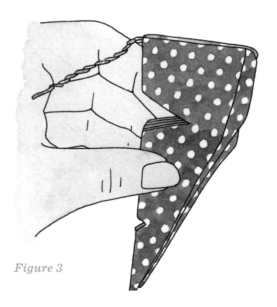

Figure 2

Figure 3

You can also use a compass to create a backing for the wall hanging.

12 / Flip the star over, and carefully unfold the pleats to form the star. At the two edges where the halves of the star need to join up, use cellophane tape to secure the pleats together (**Figure 4**).

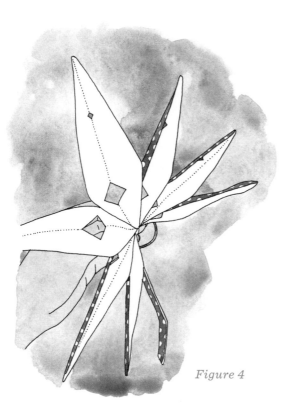

Figure 4

13 / Set the star down on a work surface with the patterned mountain folds facing up. Working with four to five folds at a time, paint a thin amount of decoupage medium on each mountain fold. Dust with gold glitter, and tap off the excess. Allow to dry. Once dry, paint over all of the glitter with a thin coat of decoupage medium. Set aside to dry.

14 / Once all glue is dry, line up the accordion star on top of the accordion circle. Thread the floral wire at the back of the star through the center of the circle.

15 / Leave wire ends loose at the back of the accordion circle to use as a hanging tool. Simply secure the wire with a small dot of hot glue where it runs through the paper.

Materials & Tools

Pencil

1 sheet tracing paper

Scissors

1 piece 3″ × 3″ cardboard (an old cereal box is perfect)

2 sheets 12″ x 12″ brown cardstock

Small paint brush

Black paint

Black glitter

Decoupage medium

Ruler

⅛″ strips of red and green quilling paper

Slotted quilling tool

Corkboard

Toothpick

Tacky glue

⅛″ strips of yellow quilling paper

Quilling circle sizer

Quilling tool

Washi tape (¼″ wide)

Craft knife

⅛″ hole punch

Red-and-white-striped baker's twine

Gingerbread Man
GARLAND

designed by ANASTASIA BOSAKOWSKI

Do you know why these gingerbread men are so happy? It's because they're made out of paper so I can't eat them! These cheery little guys look adorable on a Christmas tree. They're easy to make, and meticulous quilled details are rewarding to create. If you don't own a slotted quilling tool, vintage buttons and painted-on smiles work just as well to decorate these gingerbread men!

Instructions

1 / Using a pencil, trace the gingerbread man template (see page 134) onto the tracing paper, making sure to include the holes for the buttons, hands, eyes, and mouth. Transfer the design onto the cardboard, and cut out. Be sure to cut out the holes for the buttons, eyes, mouth, and hand holes. This will be your stencil.

2 / Trace around the stencil on brown cardstock 16 times.

3 / Cut out the gingerbread men. Transfer the placement of the buttons, eyes, mouth, and hands, but do not cut these out.

4 / One gingerbread man at a time, put a dot of paint for each eye, sprinkle with black glitter, and turn completely upside down to keep the paint from running. Tap off the excess, and allow to dry. When dry, lightly coat the glitter with decoupage medium to seal it. Repeat for all 16 gingerbread men.

5 / While the eyes dry, make the buttons. Using the ruler, measure and cut 48 lengths of quilling paper 6" long, 24 red and 24 green. One at a time, slide the quilling tool onto the paper so that it comes flush with the end of the strip of paper. Pressing into the corkboard, twirl the quilling tool to wind the paper around it until all 6" are wound on. You don't need to make it perfectly tight; a little bit of slack looks nice. Use a toothpick to put a drop of glue onto the end of the strip to secure the coil. Hold for about 10 seconds for the glue to set, then pull out the quilling tool and set aside. Repeat for all 48 strips.

6 / Pick up one gingerbread man, and place a small dot of glue onto each marking you made for the buttons. Press a quilled button lightly into the glue to attach. Repeat for each gingerbread man.

TIP

I gave each gingerbread man either red or green buttons. Feel free to mix them up with alternating colors!

7 / While the quilled buttons dry, make the mouths. Cut 16 lengths of yellow quilling paper 6" long. Place the quilling circle sizer on the corkboard. Slide the quilling tool onto the paper so that it comes flush with the end of the strip. Place the tool down onto the corkboard in the center of the #2 (⅝") hole. Twirl all of the paper onto the quilling tool, but don't do it tightly. Release the coil of paper so that it expands out to fill in the entire #2 circle. Gently pull off the quilling tool. You might need to push the quilling paper lightly with the tool to ensure that the outer edge of the paper circle reaches to the edge of the circle tool. The rest of the paper will spiral inward.

8 / Use a toothpick to glue the loose end of the outer circle. Gently pull the paper off the circle tool. After about a minute, pinch into the circle to make one corner of the smile. Pinch the opposite side of the circle to make the other. Press with your fingers to shape into a crescent shape. Repeat to make all 16 mouths.

9 / Dab a small bit of glue on the underside of each mouth and lightly place each onto the gingerbread man where you marked. Hold each in place for about 10 seconds to set.

10 / Apply strips of washi tape to the arms and legs of the gingerbread men, using the image to the right as a guide. Use your craft knife to neatly trim any overhanging edges.

11 / Using the markings you made, punch a ⅛" hole in each hand. Cut about 4 feet of striped baker's string, and string the gingerbread men onto the string. Trim off any excess string, and tie a loop at either end of the garland so you can hang it on a branch of your Christmas tree!

Materials & Tools

Pencil

1 sheet tracing paper

Scissors

Cardboard (an old cereal box is perfect)

6 sheets 12" × 12" patterned scrapbook paper in different colors

Bone folder

Small paint brush

White glue

Glitter, in six colors to match the scrapbook paper

Decoupage medium

Glue stick

⅛" hole punch

Gold thread

TIP *To get more mileage out of your craft, tie a separate string onto each crafted ornament, and gift them individually to many different friends.*

3D Vintage Ornament
GARLAND

designed by ANASTASIA BOSAKOWSKI

This multipurpose garland is a festive touch for your tree and can add a little joy to any room from the kitchen to the office! Used as a gift topper, this project can be enjoyed many times over by friends and family—first, as they open a stunning package, and then year after year as they use the garland to decorate their homes.

Instructions

1 / Using a pencil, trace each of the three 3D vintage ornament templates (see page 134) onto tracing paper. Using scissors, cut out the shapes from the tracing paper, and trace around them onto the cardboard. Cut out the cardboard shapes: These are your stencils.

2 / Choose two patterned scrapbook papers, and trace around template A six times on each sheet. Cut out all 12 outlines.

3 / Repeat step 2 with templates B and C (36 total cutouts). With small scissors, trim off any irregularities from each shape.

4 / Fold each cutout in half vertically, using a bone folder to make crisp folds.

5 / Unfold the cutouts. Paint around the edge of the patterned or colored side of the cutouts with a small amount of white glue. Gently sprinkle the glue with glitter, and tap off the excess. Allow to dry.

6 / Paint a thin layer of decoupage medium over the glitter on each cutout. Allow to dry.

> **TIP**
>
> *You can choose different colors of glitter to match each ornament's patterning, or you can use gold or silver for them all to create a cohesive look!*

7 / Fold each cutout along its crease, ensuring that the glittered side of the ornament is hidden on the inside of the fold.

> **TIP**
>
> *Each garland requires six cutouts from the same template to assemble. Make the garland from the same color for a classic look, or combine two patterned papers for an original look!*

8 / Select six cutouts from template A, and stack the folded templates. If you would like to combine two colored or patterned papers into one topper, plan out the order of colors now.

9 / Pick up the top cutout from the stack, and coat half of the folded cutout with stick glue, from the fold to the edges. When applying the glue, make sure to work with only half of the cutout, on the outer (wrong) side of the paper!

10 / Take the next folded cutout in the stack, and press it onto the glued half of the first cutout, carefully aligning both and then firmly pressing down (**Figure 1**).

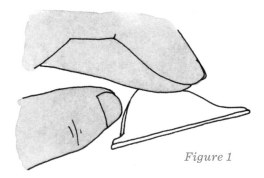

Figure 1

11 / You should now be holding two folded cutouts glued together. Next, coat the top folded cutout in your hand with stick glue.

12 / Repeat steps 10 and 11 five more times. You should now have six templates glued together in a folded stack. Press down and hold for a few seconds to allow the glue to set (Figure 2).

13 / To create a hole for hanging, punch through the top of the stack with the hole punch.

14 / Apply some glue to the top of the folded stack. Unfold the pages until the top piece meets the bottom, and press them together to complete the ornament. You should now have a three-dimensional, semi-spherical topper (Figure 3).

15 / Repeat steps 8 through 14 for each of the remaining cutout shapes.

16 / To create a garland, string all six ornaments onto a length of gold thread. Hang on your tree, or use a bow knot to attach to presents.

Figure 2

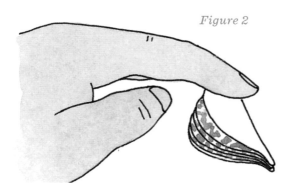

TIP

If you would like to add additional glitter to the ornaments, use white glue to repeat step 5 and add additional embellishment where desired. Cut a 7" piece of gold thread to hang the ornament while the glitter dries. Make sure to coat with another layer of decoupage medium!

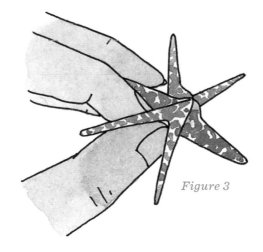

Figure 3

Materials & Tools

3 sheets 12″ × 12″ green cardstock

Scissors

Small flat paint brush

White glue

Gold glitter

¼″ double-sided tape (optional)

Gloss decoupage medium

#8 flat paint brush

1 sheet 12″ × 12″ red cardstock

Guillotine cutter (or scissors and ruler)

Tacky glue

2 sheets 12″ × 12″ striped scrapbook paper

Pencil

#1 round paint brush

Black craft paint

Black fine glitter

Circle cutter (or scissors and compass)

Glue stick

⅛″ hole punch

Gold thread

Merry Christmas
WORD GARLAND

designed by **ANASTASIA BOSAKOWSKI**

Welcome guests into your home with this cheery banner. Feel free to use your favorite greeting: "**NOEL**" will result in a speedily finished project, but if you have a large wall to cover, try "**WONDERFUL CHRISTMASTIME.**"

Instructions

1 / Using the word garland template (see page 135), cut out 15 banners from the green cardstock.

2 / Paint a thin layer of white glue along the bottom edges of each banner. Dust with gold glitter. Tap off the excess, and allow to dry.

3 / Brush a thin coat of decoupage medium over the glitter using a #8 flat paint brush. This will keep the glitter from flaking off. Allow to dry overnight.

4 / Using the provided template (see page 135) and a guillotine cutter, if available, cut out 15 strips from the red cardstock. Using tacky glue, adhere these strips to the tops of the green banner pieces.

5 / Using the provided template (see page 135), cut 15 circles from the striped scrapbook paper. (Option: You can also use a circle cutter or a compass and scissors to make the circles.) Using a pencil, plan out your lettering. Paint over the pencil lines using a #1 round paint brush and black paint. Immediately after painting each letter, sprinkle black glitter over the wet paint, and tap off the excess. Turn the painted lettering completely upside down before tapping off the excess glitter. This will help to prevent the paint from running. Allow to dry.

6 / Paint the back of each cutout circle with a glue stick. Center the circles on the green banner pieces, and stick them down.

7 / Using a hole punch, punch two holes in the upper corners of each banner piece. String onto gold thread and hang.

TIP

To get nice straight lines of glitter, use double-sided tape along the bottom edge of the banner. Apply the tape, remove the top protective film, sprinkle with glitter, and tap off the excess.

peeking under the tree
ornaments & tree decorations

Materials & Tools

Scissors

Guillotine cutter (optional)

Ruler

1 sheet 12″ × 12″ yellow cardstock

Self-healing cutting mat

Tacky glue

Hole punch

5″ length of gold thread

Finnish Star
TREE TOPPER

designed by **ANASTASIA BOSAKOWSKI**

This star looks complex, but with a few uniform paper strips and a simple weaving technique, a star can be created in less than an hour. Wow your friends by giving them stars for their own trees, or even better, teaching them how to create one themselves! Experiment by working with strips of multiple widths and colors, or adjust the space between the woven strips for an entirely new look.

Instructions

1 / Cut 12 (¾" × 12") strips from yellow cardstock.

2 / Lay out six strips onto the cutting mat, ensuring that each strip is separated by a ¼" gap, and weave together (**Figure 1**). Secure all strips with tacky glue. Allow glue to dry.

3 / You will notice that the woven square now has 12 tabs (labeled in **Figure 1**). Lift tabs C and D, line up their corners to form a neat point, and secure with tacky glue (**Figure 2**). Repeat for tabs F and G, I and J, and L and A (**Figure 3**).

4 / Repeat steps 2 and 3 with the remaining six strips. You will now have two identical star shapes.

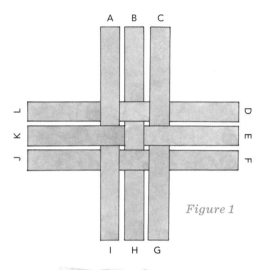

Figure 1

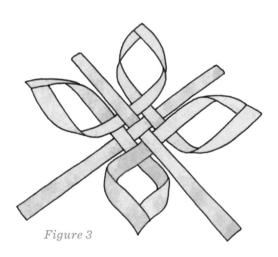

Figure 3

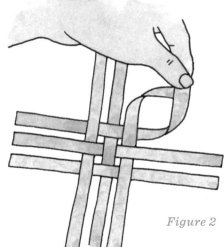

Figure 2

5 / Align one star face down on top of the other star. Make sure that the glued loops of the top piece sit over the unglued tabs of the bottom piece. Pull each tab through its corresponding loop (**Figure 4**).

6 / Working with the four loops that are flush with the cutting mat, apply a drop of glue to the point of each loop, then press the strip down on top of it. The strip will extend out beyond the point of the loop (**Figure 5**). Trim the excess paper, following the shape of the star's point (**Figure 6**). Flip the star over, and repeat with the other four loops.

7 / When the star is completely dry, gently place it onto the top of your tree. To hang, use a hole punch to create a hole in one of the star's points. Thread a 5" length of gold thread through the punched hole, and secure it with a double knot.

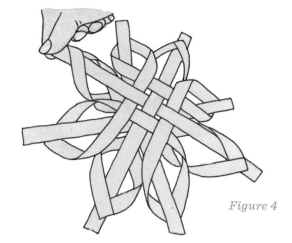

Figure 4

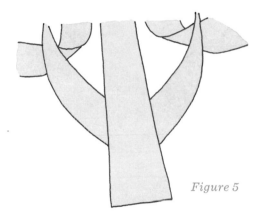

Figure 5

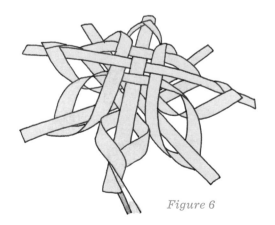

Figure 6

Materials & Tools

Pencil

1 sheet tracing paper

1 sheet 12″ × 12″ aqua cardstock

1 sheet 12″ × 12″ cobalt blue cardstock

Craft knife

Self-healing cutting mat

Scissors

Small paint brush

Tacky glue

Dark blue glitter

Bone folder

Light blue glitter

Decoupage medium

1 sheet 12″ × 12″ orange cardstock (you'll only need a small portion)

Ruler

Orange superfine glitter

Black marker

Large-eyed needle

Gold string

Bird of Paradise
ORNAMENT

designed by **ANASTASIA BOSAKOWSKI**

Birds brighten dreary winter landscapes with rare flashes of color. This little bird is loosely based on a robin, but I took the opportunity to use some of my favorite colors. Brighten your tree with a welcome surprise—a colorful bird based on nature or your imagination!

Instructions

1 / Using a pencil and tracing paper, transfer the provided bird of paradise templates (see page 136) to the indicated colored cardstock. Trace the body of the bird, the smaller wing template, and the larger tail template onto aqua cardstock, and cut out using a craft knife and cutting mat or scissors. Trace the larger wings and smaller tail template onto the cobalt blue cardstock and cut out.

2 / Using a small paint brush, apply a thin line of tacky glue along the edges of the wings, and dust with dark blue glitter. Tap off the excess, and set aside to dry.

3 / Using a bone folder, gently crease both tail pieces vertically down the center. Working on the outside of the tail (with the crease pointing upward, toward you) paint a border of tacky glue along the edges of both tail pieces, dust with dark blue glitter, and tap off the excess. Paint more tacky glue inside the border you just made on the aqua tail piece. Dust with light blue glitter, and tap off the excess. Let all of the pieces dry.

4 / Once the glitter is dry, paint a thin amount of decoupage medium over all of the cardstock, including the glitter. Allow to dry.

5 / Trace the template (see page 136) for the bird's belly out of orange paper.

6 / Fold down the tabs on the bird's body (**Figure 1**), and coat them with a thin layer of glue. Press the two sides of the bird's body together. The entire underside of the bird should be open (**Figure 2**). Allow the glue to dry.

7 / Take the orange bird belly, and place it so that the tabs are facing you. Fold the tabs upward so that they are standing perpendicular to the body. With your fingers, press the belly into a slightly rounded shape that echoes the shape of the bird's body (**Figure 3**). Place a bit of glue on each tab, and slide the belly into the bird's body with the tabs going on the inside (**Figure 4**). The pointed end should slide up under the head, and the broad part should be at the back end of the bird. Don't worry about the big hole at the back of the bird; it will be covered by the tail. Wedge a finger into that hole to help finesse the belly into place.

TIP

For a natural-looking bird, curl the tips of the bird's wings and tail upward by winding the paper around a pencil. If you curl up the tips of the bird's wings, do not apply glue to the curled parts that curl away from the bird's body.

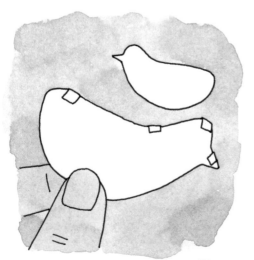

Figure 1

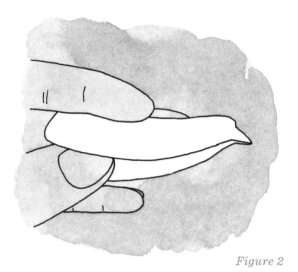

Figure 2

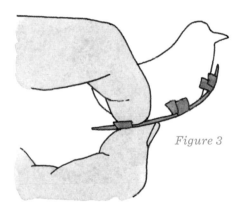

Figure 3

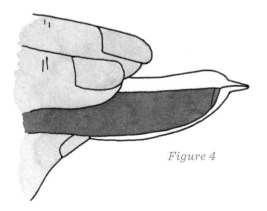

Figure 4

8 / Assemble the tail. Apply glue to the inside of the fold on the pointed tip of the smaller (cobalt blue) tail piece. Line up this smaller tail piece on top of the larger (aqua) tail piece, and press them together. Set aside.

9 / Assemble the wings. Apply glue to the underside of the smaller (cobalt) wing cutouts. Line them up on top of the larger (aqua) wing cutouts, and press them together. Next, apply glue to the entire backs (or portions, if you decided to add curls) of the wings, and attach the wings to the body, using the photo as a guide.

10 / Glue the tail onto the body, using the photo as a guide. The fold of the tail should neatly rest over the body of the bird.

11 / Paint over the beak with a thin layer of tacky glue, being sure to cover the edges of the paper, and sprinkle with orange glitter. Tap off the excess, and let dry. Paint on a second coat of glue, and dust with glitter again. Allow to dry. Finally, paint over the glitter with a thin layer of decoupage medium.

12 / Use a black marker to draw on the eye.

13 / Thread a needle with a 10" length of gold string. Push the needle up under the tail into the cavity of the bird so that it comes out through the seam in the bird's back. Hold one end of the string so it stays under the tail, and pull the rest through the top of the bird's back so that one end of the string is under the bird and the other above. Pinch the string above the bird's neck to create a loop, and run the needle back through the seam in the bird's back and below the tail. With both ends of the string coming out the bottom of the bird, tie a knot. Clip off excess string. Gently pull the loop sticking out of the top of the bird upward so that the knot rises up into the cavity of the bird.

Materials & Tools

Scissors

Circle cutter (optional)

Compass, craft knife, self-healing cutting mat (optional)

2 sheets 12″ × 12″ scrapbook paper (more if you want to use a mix of papers)

Bone folder

Pencil

Ballpoint glue pen

Cellophane tape

Tapestry needle that the hanging string fits through

Embroidery floss to hang the ornament

2 beads about ¼″ in diameter that the tapestry needle fits through

Polish Star
ORNAMENTS

designed by ANASTASIA BOSAKOWSKI

These impressive ornaments seem to come together through magic! They begin with simple, two-dimensional circles of paper, and bloom into fabulous stars in a flash.

Instructions

1 / Using the provided Polish star templates and scissors, cut out 10 circles from the scrapbook paper.

You can also use a circle cutter or a compass, craft knife, and self-healing mat to create the circles.

Figure 1

2 / Working with one circle at a time, and working on the back of the paper, cut along the perforated lines indicated in the template, creating eight "petals." Gently fold each petal in half, using a bone folder to create a crease at the center of each petal (**Figure 1**).

3 / Continuing to work on the back of the paper (patterned side down), place the tip of a pencil into the crease at the edge of a petal. Roll the paper around the tip of the pencil, creating a cone. Roll the left side in, then draw a thin line of glue along the edge of the right side, and roll it in to meet the left corner. Hold in place for about 5 seconds to secure (**Figure 2**).

4 / Continue to create a cone for each "petal" until all eight points are complete (**Figure 3**).

5 / Put a small piece of cellophane tape in the center of the circle. Pierce it with the tapestry needle where all of the radii converge, and set aside.

6 / Repeat steps 2 through 5 nine more times.

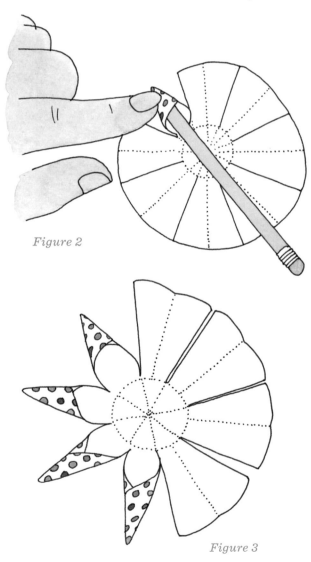

Figure 2

Figure 3

7 / Thread a tapestry needle with a 12" piece of embroidery floss. String a bead onto the floss, but don't tie a knot in the end of the floss. Instead, thread the end of the floss through the tapestry needle as well, so that you have the two loose ends on one side of the needle, and the bead on the other. Even the string up so that the bead is at the center (**Figure 4**).

8 / Stack all of the completed stars, ensuring that the bottom star has its patterned side facing down, and the other 9 stars have their pattern facing up. Beginning at the bottom of the stack, thread the needle through the center hole of each star (**Figure 4**). To get them to fit nicely together, shift each one so that the points of one star sit between the points of the star below it (**Figure 5**).

9 / Once you have all ten stars strung onto the embroidery floss, slip the second bead onto the needle, and nestle it against the top star (**Figure 6**).

10 / Pull the tapestry needle off of the floss, and gently pull the two loose ends of the embroidery floss away from each other. This will cause the top bead to push down on the stack and slowly pull them into a ball shape. Tie the strings into a tight knot, securing the bead against the ornament. Tie the ends of the strings together to create a hanging loop and trim.

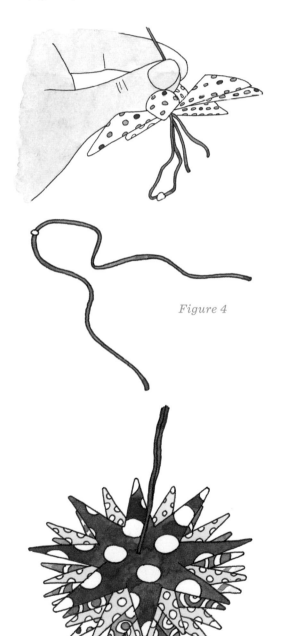

Figure 4

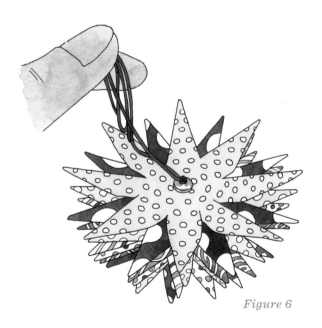

Figure 6

Figure 5

Materials & Tools

Scissors

Ruler (optional)

Craft knife (optional)

Self-healing cutting mat (optional)

Guillotine cutter (optional)

1 sheet 12" × 12" cardstock (you'll need much less)

⅛" hole punch

¼" double-sided tape

Tinsel glitter

Small paint brush

Decoupage medium

Needle

Embroidery floss

2 crystal beads with a hole that the beading needle will pass through

Art Deco Bulb

PAPER STRIP ORNAMENTS

designed by ELLEN DEAKIN

Reminiscent of antique glass bulbs, these ornaments are simple to make and impossible to break! Made from strips of paper in multiple lengths, these ornaments naturally bulge out into the perfect shape. This easy project is perfect to craft with kids!

Instructions

1 / Using the star and spiral ornament templates provided on page 138 and scissors, cut two strips of template A, two of template B, two of template C, and one of template D. Make sure to transfer the marker for the hole punch onto each strip. Punch a hole in each strip as indicated, excluding template A.

> **TIP**
>
> *Alternatively, you can use a ruler, craft knife, and cutting mat or a guillotine cutter to make the strips for step 1.*

2 / Take the two longest strips (template A), and adhere a strip of double-sided tape down the center, lengthwise. Sprinkle tinsel glitter along the tape, tap off the excess, then paint a very thin coat of decoupage medium over the glitter, and allow to dry. This may take a few hours or overnight.

3 / Once the decoupage medium is dry, use the ⅛" hole punch to punch a hole as indicated in the template.

4 / Lay one of the glittered strips from template A with the glitter side down. On top of it stack the strips in this order: template B, template C, template D, template C, template B. Finish with the last glittered strip of template A, making sure that the glitter side faces up. You will have sandwiched all of the strips, with the longest strips on the outside and the shortest in the middle of the stack. Adjust the strips so that the hole punch at the bottom of each strip is overlapped (the tops of each strip will be at different heights).

5 / Thread the needle with a 12" length of embroidery floss. Pass it through the hole at the bottom of each strip, leaving 6" of embroidery floss on either side of the stack of strips. Remove the needle, and tightly tie a double knot, securing the strips together.

6 / Thread both ends of the embroidery floss through the needle. String one of the beads onto the needle, sliding it up to the paper strips, and secure with two tight overhand knots (add a few more if the knot is thin enough to slip through the bead). Trim off excess floss.

7 / Repeat steps 5 and 6 for the top of the strips. In order to align the hole punches at the top of each strip, you will need to allow the longer strips to bow out. This will provide the shape of the ornament. Don't trim the excess after you tie the knots under the bead. Instead, tie the very ends together to form a loop to hang the ornament.

> **TIP**
>
> *You can pinch the bowed-out center of the longest strips to give your ornament a more dramatic shape.*

Materials & Tools

Ruler

1 sheet 12″ × 12″ scrapbook paper

Scissors

Bone folder

Tacky glue

Clothes pins

1/8″ hole punch

7″ length gold string

TIP *You need to use paper printed on both sides if the back will be visible.*

Accordion-Fold Star
ORNAMENT

designed by ANASTASIA BOSAKOWSKI

These stars are simple to make, so I suggest creating a bunch of them! It's simple to change the size—just start with smaller squares of paper. As shown, they're a wee bit large for a tree (or at least, my tree), but I like to hang them off drawer knobs to dress up the sideboard and use suction cups to hang them on windows. Also, starting with 6″ squares makes efficient use of 12″ squares of paper.

Instructions

1 / With the ruler, measure four 6" squares from the 12" × 12" scrapbook paper. (You will only need three.) Cut out three of the squares with scissors.

2 / Fold each of the three squares in half, corner to corner, to form a triangle. Cut along the folds. You'll now have 6 triangles.

3 / Place one triangle on the table in front of you with the longest side up and the point down (it'll look like an arrowhead pointing at your chest). Fold the left corner over to the right corner to create a crease down the center of the triangle. Unfold. Now, fold the bottom point of the triangle up to the top of the triangle, being sure the point is centered on the crease you just made. Press with a bone folder. Fold the bottom edge up to meet the top edge once more, and press with a bone folder. You will now have two horizontal folds in your triangle. Fold the bottom edge to meet the top edge, and press with a bone folder two more times. Unfold. You will now have four horizontal creases in your triangle, separating your triangle into equal eighths. Refold these creases accordion-style, folding each crease in the opposite direction of the crease below it. You'll end up with a long, thin strip (**Figure 1**).

Figure 1

4 / Position the resulting strip in front of you so that the little triangle in the center is pointing up. If you're working with paper printed on one side, be sure that the printed side of the little center triangle is showing. Put a drop of glue on that center triangle, and fold the strip in half. You should be able to follow your original vertical fold line. Use a clothespin to hold the fold in place while the glue dries.

5 / Repeat steps 3 and 4 for all of the triangles. You'll end up with 6 glued strips. Arrange these V-shaped, folded strips so that they're in a circle, with the open end of the V facing out and the printed side of the paper facing up (**Figure 2**).

Figure 2

6 / Apply a very thin line of glue to the outer edge of each V, and attach that V to the V beside it.

7 / Once the glue is dry, punch a hole at the top of one of the points of the star and thread with a 7" length of gold string for hanging. Tie a knot, and you're ready to hang your star.

Materials & Tools

Pencil

1 sheet tracing paper

1 sheet 12″ × 12″ dark red cardstock

Scissors

¼″ double-sided tape

Craft knife

Self-healing cutting mat

Small paint brush

Tacky glue

Silver glitter

Decoupage medium

1 sheet 12″ × 12″ green cardstock (you'll only need a small portion)

Bone folder

Glue stick

Ruler

Dark red embroidery floss

1 sheet 12″ × 12″ yellow cardstock (you'll only need a small portion)

Santa's Sleigh
ORNAMENT

designed by **ANASTASIA BOSAKOWSKI**

Well here's something we'd all like to see parked on our roof on Christmas Eve! This sled is a sweet addition to your tree, but you could easily make a bunch of them and use them as place card holders at Christmas dinner! Just write your guests' names in silver marker on the side of each sleigh.

Instructions

1 / Use the pencil and tracing paper and the provided Santa's sleigh template (see page 139) to transfer each side of the sleigh onto red cardstock. Cut out with scissors.

2 / Place a piece of ¼" double-sided tape on each side of the sleigh, right above the holes for the sleigh runners (the tape will give a crisp, straight line). Lay the cutout on the cutting mat to trim off the excess tape with a craft knife. Using a small paint brush, paint a thin coat of tacky glue over the rest of the sleigh runners. Peel off the protective film from the tape, and sprinkle silver glitter over the tape and glue. Tap off the excess, and set the pieces aside to dry.

3 / Once dry, apply a thin coat of decoupage medium over the glitter. Allow to dry.

4 / Transfer the provided present template (see page 139) to the green cardstock.

5 / Using a bone folder, crease along each dotted line indicated on the template. Fold along the creases, and secure the edges of the box using a glue stick. Set aside to dry.

6 / Use a ruler to measure and cut an 18" length of embroidery floss. Wrap it around the box as you would with a real gift. Tie a simple bow, and trim off any excess length.

7 / Repeat steps 4 through 6 with yellow cardstock.

8 / Transfer the provided template for the bottom of the sleigh (see page 139) to red cardstock, and cut out.

9 / Using the sides of the sleigh as your guide, gently curve the bottom of the sleigh so it will fit against both sides. The bottom will sit just above the glittered portion of the sleigh pieces. Bend up the tabs on the sleigh's bottom. Apply a bit of tacky glue to the outside of the tabs. Gently press each side of the sleigh against the tabs on either side of the sleigh's bottom. Press into place, and hold for about 30 seconds.

10 / When the sleigh is completely dry, place the gifts inside. See the photo at right for their arrangement. Use a drop of tacky glue to secure them into place.

Templates

Poinsettia Gift Topper

(Photocopy at 133% to enlarge)

Old Book Gift Topper

(Photocopy at 133% to enlarge)

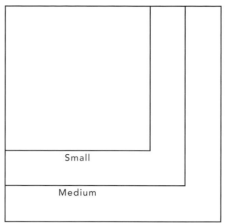

Book page templates

Small

Medium

Large

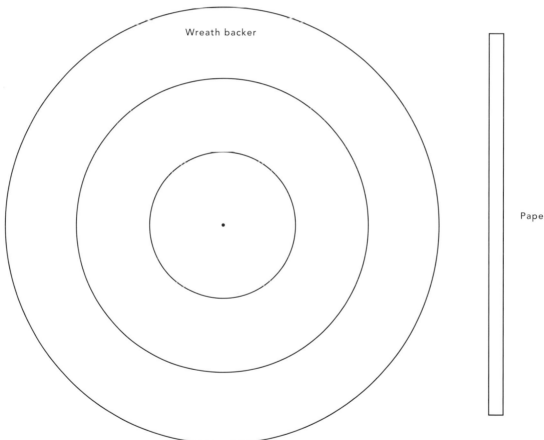

Wreath backer

Paper strip

Festive Trio Cards

(Photocopy at 100%)

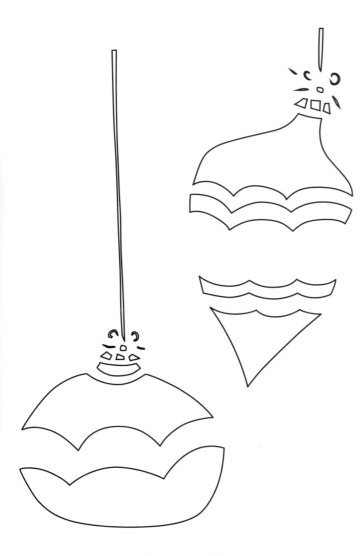

Ornament card

Be Merry card

Merry + Bright card

Raccoon Card

(Photocopy at 100%)

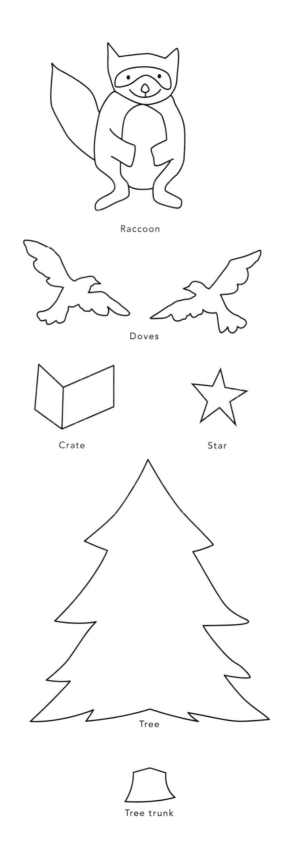

Raccoon

Doves

Crate

Star

Tree

Tree trunk

Paper Stag

(Photocopy at 100%)

Welcome Home Glass Dome

(Photocopy at 200% to enlarge)

Wolf Bear, Polar Bear & Tree Silhouettes

(Photocopy at 133% to enlarge)

Stand

3D Tree Centerpiece

(Photocopy at 400% to enlarge)

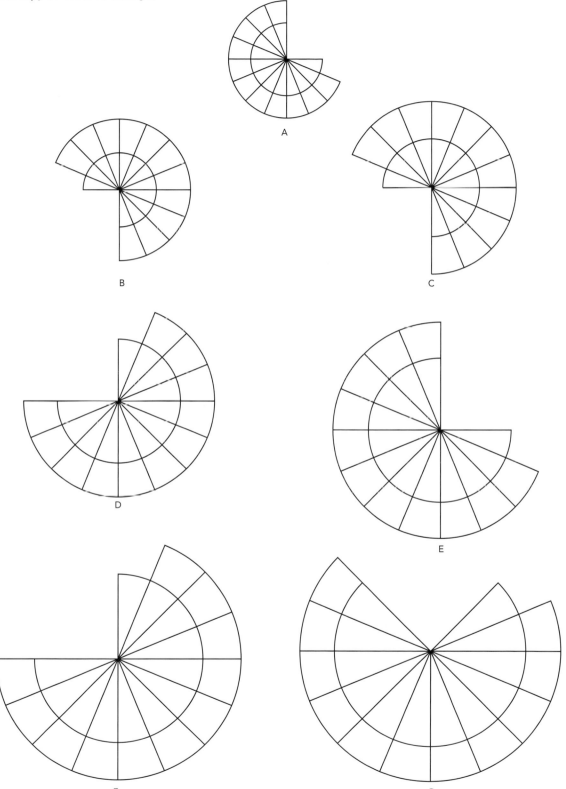

Noel Luminaries

(Photocopy at 133% to enlarge)

Noel Luminaries (continued)

(Photocopy at 100%)

Vellum rectangle

Pinecone Place Card Holder

(Photocopy at 100%)

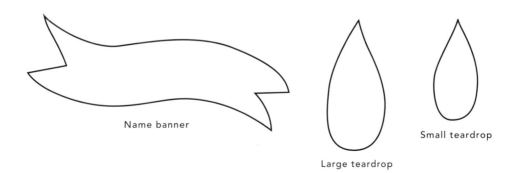

Name banner

Large teardrop

Small teardrop

Reindeer Centerpiece

(Photocopy at 133% to enlarge)

fold and glue back to back

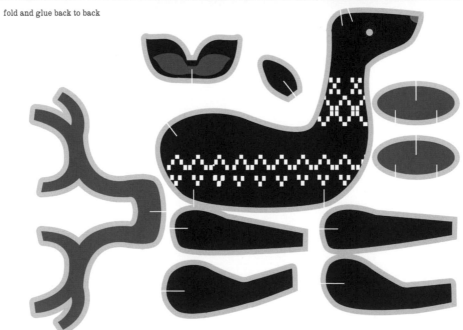

Reindeer Centerpiece (continued)

(Photocopy at 133% to enlarge)

fold and glue back to back

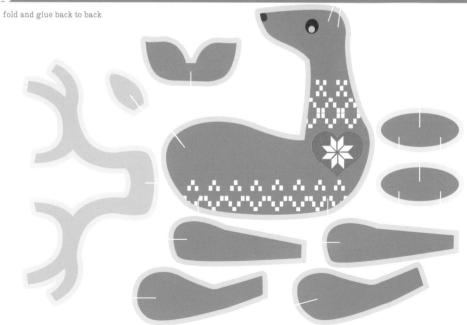

Reindeer Centerpiece (continued)

(Photocopy at 133% to enlarge)

fold and glue back to back

fold here

fold and hang
around neck.
Glue the back of
the hearts together.

Advent Calendar

(Photocopy at 100%)

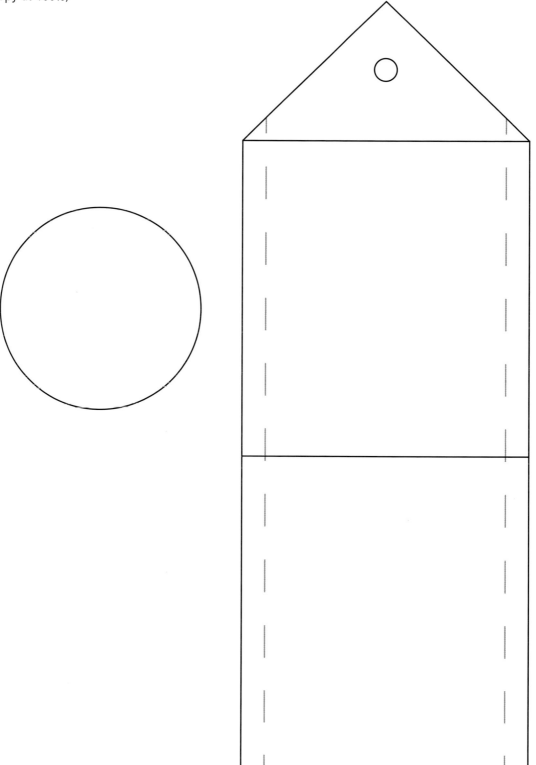

Book Lover's Wreath

(Photocopy at 133% to enlarge)

Book Lover's Wreath (continued)

(Photocopy at 133% to enlarge)

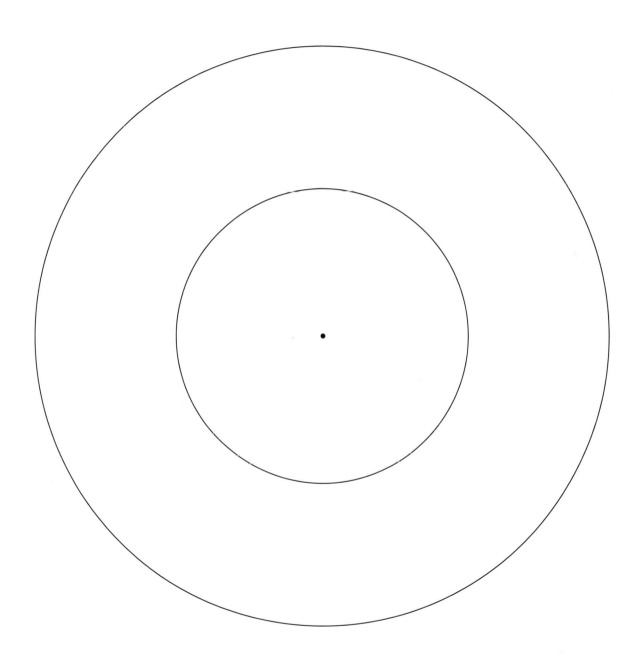

Accordion-Fold Star Decoration

(Photocopy at 133% to enlarge)

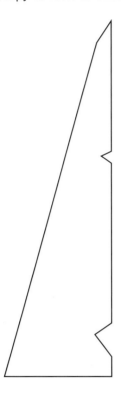

Gingerbread Man Garland

(Photocopy at 133% to enlarge)

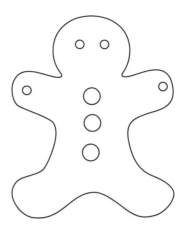

3D Vintage Ornament Garland

(Photocopy at 133% to enlarge)

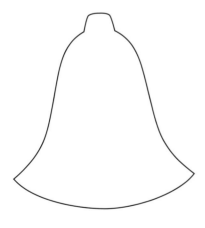
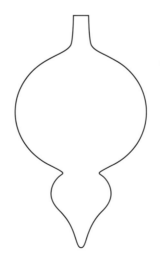
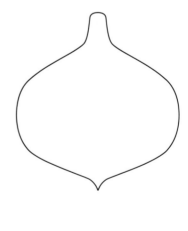

Merry Christmas Word Garland

(Photocopy at 133% to enlarge)

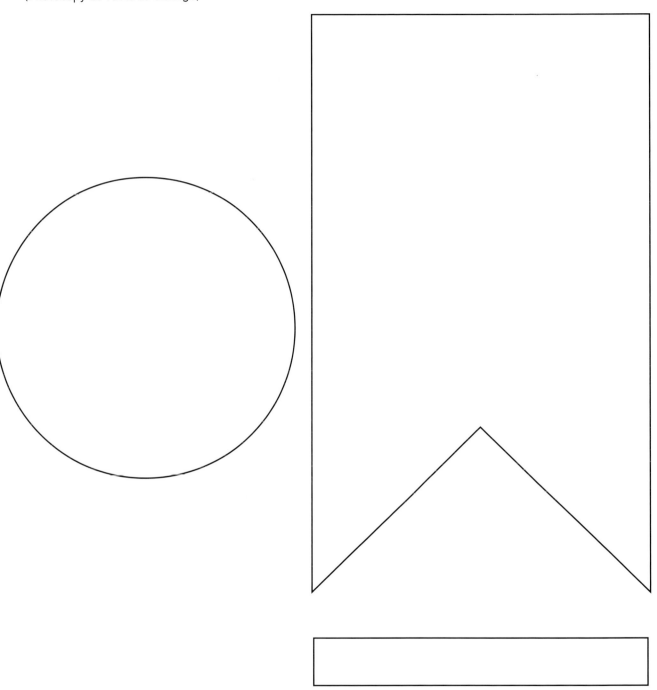

Bird of Paradise Ornament

(Photocopy at 100%)

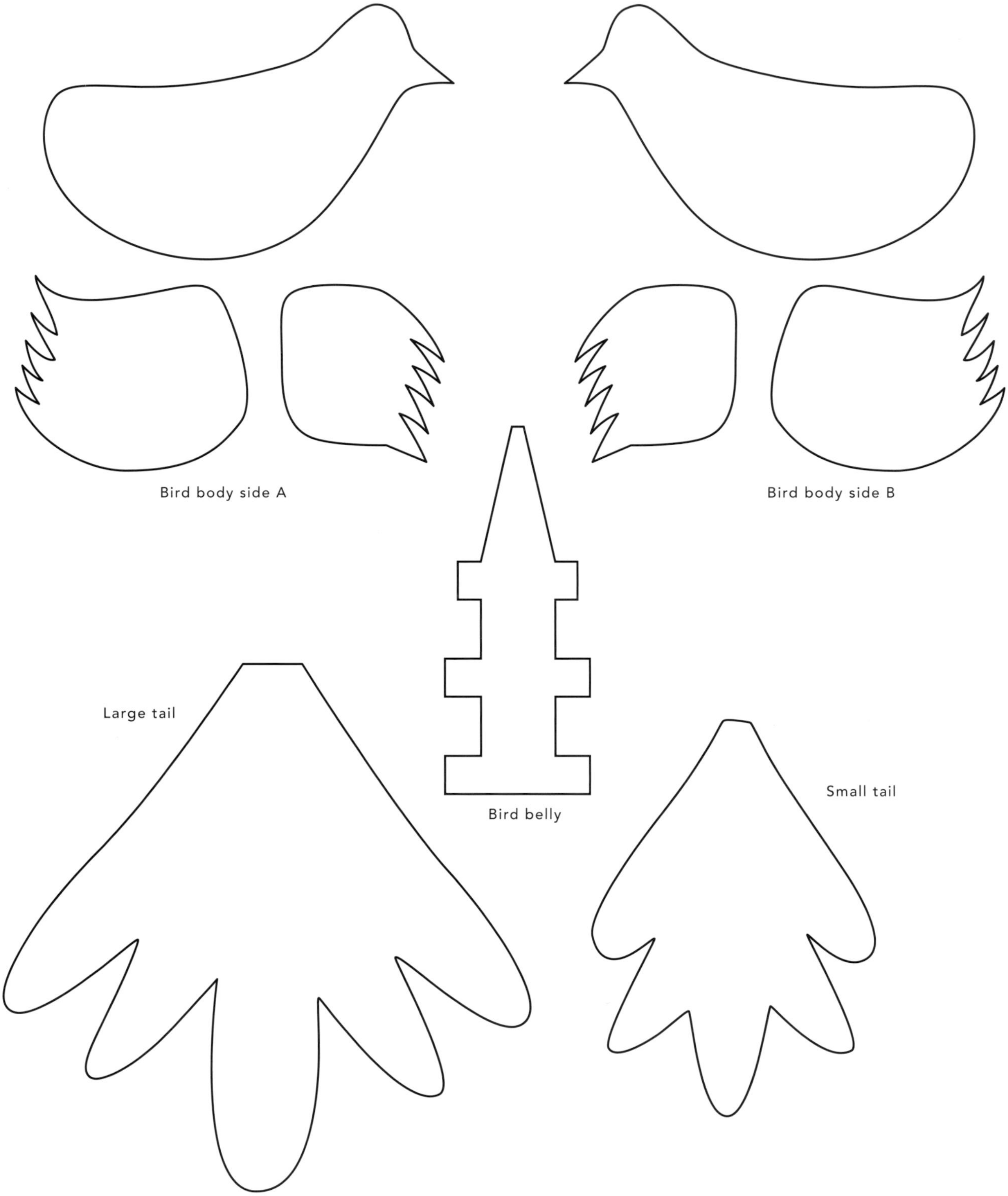

Bird body side A

Bird body side B

Large tail

Bird belly

Small tail

Polish Star

(Photocopy at 100%)

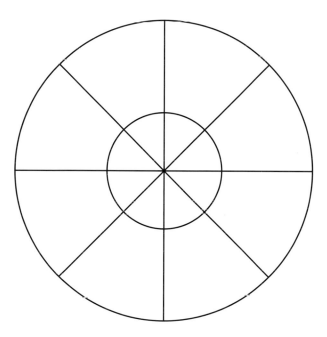

Art Deco Bulb Ornament

(Photocopy at 100%)

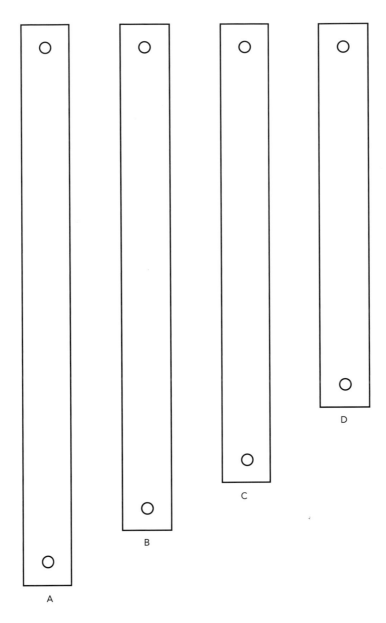

Santa's Sleigh Ornament

(Photocopy at 100%)

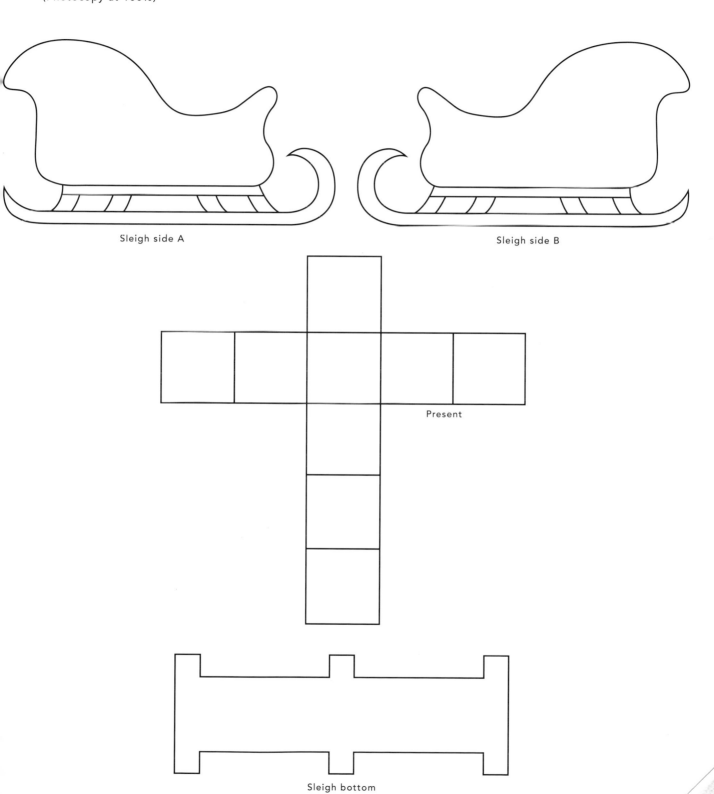

Sleigh side A

Sleigh side B

Present

Sleigh bottom

About the Contributors

ANASTASIA BOSAKOWSKI

Lifelong crafter Anastasia Bosakowski calls herself a "Jack of all trades, master of some." Beyond playing with paper, she crochets, cross stitches, makes jewelry, sews, and tries pretty much anything that gives her an excuse to collect more crafting supplies. Since 2008 she has been the editor of Crafter's Choice Book Club. Her other passions are David Bowie, European travel, medieval history, and greyhound rescue. She lives in New York City with Loki, her feline roommate. She dedicates her projects to her parents, William and Geraldine Bosakowski, who taught her that art was something to both love and make.

ELLEN DEAKIN

Happythought founders Ellen Deakin and Harry Olden met at the Glasgow School of Art. After a decade of working in the design and music industry, they launched Happythought, an online store and blog full of craft ideas and fun printable paper crafts. They are currently based in Chile with their two young children Harvey and Missy, who are a constant source of inspiration and the perfect guinea pigs (and sometime models) for new creations and craft tutorials.

At Happythought, the emphasis is on producing paper craft templates that are lovely to look at and easy to make, with a minimum of fuss and a maximum of fun. All Happythought, printables can be made using scissors and a glue stick.

SILVINA DE VITA

Silvina De Vita is a designer and illustrator from Argentina living in London. After experimenting with different materials, she fell in love with paper and the vast number of possibilities it offers. She makes paper cut illustrations that feature the stories of people she encounters. She uses paper cutting as a kind of meditation. Her work has been featured in magazines, books, and exhibitions around London. You can see more of her work at www.silvinadevita.com

ALEXANDRA HARRISON

Ali Harrison is the owner of the Light and Paper Shop in Toronto, Ontario. She has always loved creating art, but didn't discover her passion for paper cutting until 2012. Ali loves being able to create paper cutting art in large and small form, everything from large-scale pieces that span an entire wall to simple cards to give a friend. Ali is excited that in addition to sharing her work, she can inspire others to try their hand at their own paper creations. See more of her creations at LightandPaperShop.Com and on Etsy.

Index

note: Page numbers in *italics* indicate photos of individual projects. Page numbers in parentheses indicate project templates. Page numbers in **bold** indicate contributor bios.